INSPIRATION OF THE BIBLE

Inspiration of the Bible

By
B. H. CARROLL, D.D.

Compiled and Edited
By
J. B. CRANFILL

Original Introduction by
GEORGE W. TRUETT AND
L. R. SCARBOROUGH

Introduction and Notes to 1980 edition by
PAIGE PATTERSON

Thomas Nelson Publishers
Nashville

Inspiration of the Bible was
originally published in 1930.

1980 edition published by Thomas Nelson Publishers, Nashville, Tennessee.

The publisher wishes to thank Dallas Baptist
College, Dallas, Texas, for supplying the original
volume used in producing this volume.

ISBN 0-8407-5735-2

CONTENTS

FOREWORD

THE incomparable, far-famed preacher and educator, B. H. Carroll, was a man whose varied intellectual achievements were matched by pulpit prowess and administrative sagacity. No monograph of Dr. Carroll is any more crucial than this one graciously reprinted here by Thomas Nelson Publishers. And the personal testimony embodied in the sermon of Dr. Carroll is one of the most moving passages in the developing literature of the great Southwest.

Our gratitude is expressed not only to Sam Moore of Thomas Nelson for reprinting this Baptist classic at such a crucial time in our history, but also to Dr. Paige Patterson for locating the manuscript, adding explanatory footnotes, appending a new introduction, and sharing all this with our brethren. May God bless this timely reprinting to the edification of our people.

W. A. CRISWELL
Dallas, Texas
Spring, 1980

INTRODUCTION

BORN in Carroll County, Mississippi, in 1843, Benajah Harvey Carroll was not converted until he was twenty-two years of age. He was ordained at age twenty-three and became assistant pastor of the First Baptist Church in Waco, Texas, at age twenty-seven. A year later he became pastor of that great church and continued there for twenty-eight years. However, his later years were probably the most fruitful when he served as president of the Southwestern Baptist Theological Seminary, a position he held until his death in 1914.

Carroll was a man of gigantic intellect, reading extensively and retaining an overwhelming amount of information. Though he never attended a theological seminary, he was one of the greatest theologians of his generation.

This dynamic preacher had a phenomenal ability to explain and interpret even the most difficult passages in the Bible. He was fervent in his preaching and eloquent in his delivery. He was a committed prophet of God and refused to bow to the whims of men. His life exemplified Christ because he was totally committed to the authority of the Scriptures. His evangelistic zeal was prompted by a heart full of compassion and concern for the lost.

Dr. Carroll was without equal as a preacher. He was a scholarly, biblical theologian. He was a challenging teacher. He was the greatest Christian statesman Texas has ever had.

Whether thought of as an eloquent preacher, a profound theologian, or as the eminent founder of Southwestern Baptist Theological Seminary, underlying all is the clear testimony that B. H. Carroll was totally committed to the Scriptures as the very word of God.

The contribution of Benajah Harvey Carroll to the life of Baptists in America is permanently enshrined at Baylor University, in the First Baptist Church of Waco, Texas, and at Southwestern Baptist Theological Seminary in Fort Worth, Texas. However, while a few Baptists have read segments from Carroll's *An Interpretation of the English Bible*, the majority have never had the privilege of delving into some of the great preacher's insights as represented in book and sermon.

Inspiration of the Bible was a crucial work, a major concomitant in the theology of the founder of Southwestern Seminary. An idea of the importance of this book may be gleaned from the prominent names of Baptist leaders associated with the book. The incomparable J. B. Cranfill edited this 1930 edition. George W. Truett, the prestigious pastor of the First Baptist Church in Dallas, Texas, for more than forty years, and L. R. Scarborough, the man who did more than any other to fan the flames of evangelistic zeal in Texas and the West, both testify to the crucial nature of this book by appending their respective introductions.

Carroll realized that the future of the evangelistic and missionary enterprise of any denomination depends upon the solid foundations of its theology. Carroll's confidence in the full trustworthiness and impeccable veracity of the Bible formed the basis for all that he did. He knew very well that laying aside the doctrine of the inerrancy and infallibility of the Bible would spell eventual catastrophe for Baptists.

Near the time of his death, Dr. Carroll talked with L. R. Scarborough, stressing the critical nature of orthodoxy. Scarborough records these words.

B. H. Carroll, the greatest man I ever knew, as he was about to die, a few days before he died, expecting me, as he wanted me, to succeed him as president of the seminary, I was in his room one day and he pulled himself up by my chair with his hands and looked me in the face. There were times when he looked like he was forty feet high. And he looked into my face and said, "My boy, on this Hill orthodoxy, the old truth is making one of its last stands and I want to deliver to you a charge and I do it in the blood of Jesus Christ." He said, "You will be elected president of the seminary. I want you, if there ever comes heresy in your faculty, to take it to your faculty. If they won't hear you, take it to the trustees. If they won't hear you take it to the conventions that appointed them. If they won't hear you, take it to the common Baptists. They will hear you. And," he said, "I charge you in the name of Jesus Christ to keep it lashed to the old Gospel of Jesus Christ." As long as I have influence in that institution, by the grace of God I will stand by the old Book.*

Baptist people need to rediscover their heritage. The confidence that B. H. Carroll placed in Scripture will be apparent in this volume. Obviously, Cranfill, Truett, and Scarborough held the same view. Almost all Baptists affirmed the trustworthiness of the Bible in every syllable. One of the essentials for revival and evangelism in our day is a reaffirmation of this same view of the Bible—a view that was held by Jesus, Paul, Peter, and most of the Anabaptist and Baptist divines from the sixteenth century until now.

Included with this book is the republication of a masterpiece of rhetoric, Dr. Carroll's famous sermon "My Infidelity and What Became of It" (see Appendix). This sermon provides insight into the circumstances and events through

---

*L. R. Scarborough, *Gospel Messages* (Nashville: Sunday School Board of the Southern Baptist Convention, 1922), pp. 227-28.

which Dr. Carroll became an ardent advocate of the infallibility of the Bible. Our prayer to God is that the treatise and the sermon will bless the lives of saints again in this generation, even as they comforted and instructed in days gone by.

PAIGE PATTERSON, PRESIDENT
Criswell Center for Biblical Studies
Dallas, Texas
March, 1980

EDITOR'S FOREWORD

THE estimate of the character and greatness of B. H. Carroll, voiced by George W. Truett in his Introduction to this discussion of the *Inspiration of the Bible,* is neither fanciful nor exaggerated. I join him in appraising the author of this volume as the most commanding figure that has ever marched through the history of American ecclesiasticism.

For almost twelve years he was my pastor, but prior to that time I had sensed his greatness and in a limited degree had begun publishing his work. Since then it has been my happy privilege to edit four of his books, *Carroll's Sermons, Baptists and Their Doctrines, Evangelistic Sermons,* and *The River of Life.*

In addition to these books I have edited *Carroll's Interpretation of the English Bible,* comprising thirteen octavo volumes that contain luminous discussions of the Old and New Testaments.

B. H. Carroll was the founder of the Southwestern Baptist Theological Seminary and was its first President. His heart was aflame with an affectionate desire to furnish opportunity for the cultural and theological equipment of that great and loyal army of young preachers to whom had been denied the privilege of college training.

Indeed, this desire and purpose was the germ from which the Southwestern Baptist Theological Seminary came into being, and *Carroll's Interpretation of the English Bible* was and is the most edifying discussion of the Bible extant in any tongue.

B. H. Carroll was rock-ribbed in his reverent belief in God's Word, and this present discussion is the crowning expression of his unyielding faith in the oracles of God. If there was ever a time when our wobbling world needed to hear a clamant voice calling it back to the changeless verities of the Word of God, that time is now.

Due acknowledgment is herein accorded Professor J. W. Crowder, long-time student of B. H. Carroll and his loving and admiring fellow-worker, for invaluable aid in the preparation of this book. Due recognition is also given President L. R. Scarborough, successor to B. H. Carroll, for his sympathetic co-operation and his gracious words of commendation that accompany this book.

And now *Inspiration of the Bible* begins its mission to our needy world. It is so brief it can be read at one sitting and so profound that its complete study and assimilation will take an entire lifetime.

While its author was a Baptist he loomed so large that his big heart and life took in all the world.

I published his first sermon in 1884. That was forty-six years ago. I am now older than he was when he passed into rest, and I wonder, as these words are done, if my service in the editing and compilation of these works of B. H. Carroll is not my crowning contribution to the world.

J. B. CRANFILL.

Dallas, Texas.

SOME WORDS OF INTRODUCTION

IT gives me much pleasure to write these brief introductory words concerning Dr. B. H. Carroll's delayed volume on the *Inspiration of the Bible.*

Speaking quite personally, by the reader's generous forbearance, I would say that it was my privilege to know Dr. Carroll intimately for many years. It was my inexpressibly happy privilege to be a member of his household and live in his home for several years. I am more indebted to him for my reverence for God's Holy Word than I am to any other human being. His was the greatest personality I ever knew and, unlike some historic characters, he ever increasingly loomed largest to those nearest him.

During my student days at Baylor University, I was a member of his class in English Bible—the department in Baylor which afterwards eventuated in the Southwestern Baptist Theological Seminary. Much of the material in the present volume was used in his lectures to his classes in Baylor and, later, repeated to his students in the Seminary.

The chapters of this book, having thus been first delivered as lectures, appear in a flowing familiar style that adds to the interest and value of the volume. While now and then, some Greek and Latin terms are used, the greater portion of this book is clothed in direct and simple speech that all can understand. Every word in *Inspiration of the Bible* is of easy comprehension to the common mind, which adds much to its value.

Along with many other young ministers who were students in Baylor, I was privileged for four consecutive years to sit at the feet of this remarkable Bible teacher and interpreter, and regularly to hear his expositions of the Holy Scriptures. Such expositions have become more real and precious to me, with my own direct study of the Bible, through all the unfolding years. Whatever may be one's views concerning the Divine authorship and integrity of the Bible, it is my deep conviction that the candid reader anywhere and everywhere will get untold good from the reading of this volume.

I am profoundly glad that these long-delayed messages from Dr. Carroll are thus being given permanent form, and it is my earnest hope that this volume will speedily find a place in the library of preachers, teachers, and other Bible students everywhere.

The expression, "Mighty in the Scriptures," could be applied to Dr. Carroll as to few other men of his own or any other age. It will indeed be a glorious result if this volume shall be the challenge to a renewed and widespread study of the Bible. May God grant it, for His Name's sake!

GEORGE W. TRUETT.

Dallas, Texas.

A FURTHER INTRODUCTION

AMONG the many preachers and teachers who have helped me in the study of God's Word, two have the primary place—my father, Rev. George W. Scarborough, and Dr. B. H. Carroll.

Around the family fireside in a Western cow ranch and farmer's home, my father unfolded God's Word and often talked about the Bible. He preached to the cowboys of the West, and I heard him gladly. He was a doctrinal, but deeply spiritual preacher.

When I left home for Baylor University my father asked me to promise him that I would hear Dr. Carroll preach every Sunday morning and in the afternoon write him what he preached about. For four and a half years I kept this promise many Sundays. Meagre were the reports at first, but voluminous as the years went on. This great pastor of the First Baptist Church at Waco, in those four and a half years, implanted in my soul very largely my conception of the truth.

My faith is the faith of a simple, plain Baptist. I accepted from my father and Dr. Carroll the verbal inspiration of the Bible, the deity of Jesus Christ, His perfect humanity, His atoning death, His bodily resurrection, His second coming. All my studies since have confirmed the simple faith I received from them.

I greatly joy in the publication of this volume of Dr. Carroll's sermons on the inspiration of the Bible. His interpretative authority has great weight with me, but I have never had occasion to depart from his teachings on these

11

great themes. The logic, piling Scripture upon Scripture, coming from his great brain, made irresistible the force of his pronouncements.

He was the greatest preacher and the mightiest soul I ever knew.

He made deep tracks in Christ's kingdom in Texas and the South—tracks that time cannot wear out.

I trust that the messages he brings on this great theme will be quietly studied by multitudes of religious leaders, and I am sure the power of his messages will live long in their hearts and effectively in their lives.

L. R. SCARBOROUGH.

President's Office,
Southwestern Baptist Theological Seminary,
Fort Worth, Texas.

INSPIRATION OF THE BIBLE

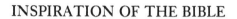

I

INSPIRATION OF THE SCRIPTURES AS BELIEVED
BY BAPTISTS

W E believe that the Holy Bible was written by men divinely inspired, and is a perfect treasure of heavenly instruction; that it has God for its author, salvation for its end, and truth without any mixture of error for its matter; that it reveals the principles by which God will judge us; and therefore is, and shall remain to the end of the world, the true centre of Christian union, and the supreme standard by which all human conduct, creeds, and opinions shall be tried."

This is the first Article of Faith of a great many Baptist churches in our Southland. The first statement is, "We believe that the Holy Bible was written by men divinely inspired." This brings us at once to the subject of the inspiration of the Scriptures. The word inspiration is derived from the Latin word *inspiro*, which means to breathe on or to breathe into. That is the literal meaning of the word.

The theological meaning is to breathe on or to breathe into for the purpose of conveying the Holy Spirit, in order that those inspired may speak or write what God would have spoken or written. That is inspiration.

A Scriptural example of this is found in John 20:22: "And when he said this he breathed on them and saith unto them, Receive ye the Holy Spirit." That gives us the true conception of inspiration. Following that, verse 23 gives the result: " Whosesoever sins ye forgive, they are forgiven unto them; whosesoever sins ye retain, they are retained." That

15

is, an inspired man can declare exactly the terms of remission of sins, and the terms upon which sins cannot be remitted, because he is speaking for God.

The book that a man, so breathed on, writes is called *theopneustos,* a Greek word meaning " God-inspired." Example:

" From a babe thou hast known the sacred writings, which are able to make thee wise unto salvation, through faith in Christ Jesus. Every scripture is inspired of God . . ."— II Tim. 3:15, 16.

After God breathed into man the Holy Spirit in order that he should accurately write the things which God wanted written, then the book that he wrote was called *theopneustos.* So that this second passage is a very important one in discussing inspiration, probably the most important in the whole Bible.

If the book is God-inspired, then it is God's book and not man's book.

Another illustration is found in the second chapter of Genesis:

"And Jehovah God formed man of the dust of the ground, and breathed into his nostrils the breath of life, and man became a living soul."

The body was present, but it was dead. It had no vitality. The distinction between a body that is in-breathed and a body that is not in-breathed is the distinction between death and life. Therefore, a man's book is a dead book. I don't care how lofty its thought, how fine its argument, or how perfect its rhetoric, the book will pass away. It has not the principle of eternal life. But books that are God-breathed are called " living oracles " (Acts 7:38). It is impossible for a God-book to die.

The oldest book that was ever God-inspired is as much living as the latest one, and it will be unto the end of time a living oracle.

But what is an oracle? In Greece there were certain shrines—certain deities—such as the oracle of Apollo at Delphi. There was a priestess that ministered at that shrine. Men would stand before her and ask a question and the priestess would fall into an ecstasy, and while in that ecstasy her answers were called oracles. Heathen oracles are all dumb, but these God-inspired oracles are living.

They are not only called living oracles, but they are called the oracles of God, as we see from Romans 3:2:

"What advantage hath the Jew? Much every way, for first of all they were entrusted with the oracles of God."

The advantage is that these Old Testament books were entrusted to them, not as man's books, but as containing the speeches of God, as well as the works of God.

Now, I will briefly set forth the inspiration of both the Old and the New Testament. II Timothy 3:15, 16, covers all the Old Testament. Paul says to Timothy: "From a babe thou hast known the sacred writings." Any other writing is what is called profane writing, not in our modern sense of profanity, but means not divine, but rather human or secular. "Thou hast known the sacred writings, which are able to make thee wise unto salvation. Every scripture is inspired of God," etc. He first speaks of the books of the Old Testament in groups, *ta hiera grammata*, the sacred writings. Then he speaks of them distributively, *pasa graphe*. Every one of these sacred writings is God-inspired.

We may stand on that one declaration to affirm the inspiration of every one of the Old Testament books.

Another passage bearing on Old Testament inspiration is II Peter 1:20:

"No prophecy of scripture is of private interpretation. For no prophecy ever came by the will of man: but men spake from God, being moved by the Holy Spirit."

Here again is the idea of inspiration. An inspired man, when he speaks, does not speak his will; when he writes, he does not write his will, but he speaks and writes for God, being moved by the Holy Spirit.

Now let us take up the New Testament. In John 14:26 we find that a promise was made, before inspiration was given, that they should be inspired:

"But the Comforter, even the Holy Spirit, whom the Father will send in my name, he shall teach you all things, and bring to your remembrance all that I said unto you."

Again in 16:12, 13:

"I have yet many things to say unto you, but ye cannot bear them now. Howbeit when he, the Spirit of truth, is come he shall guide you into all the truth; for he shall not speak from himself; but what things soever he shall hear, these shall he speak; and he shall declare unto you the things that are to come."

That is, Christ in His lifetime did not complete the revealed truth. They were not prepared to receive it all. But He made provision for the revealing of the truth by promising the Holy Spirit who would teach them all that it was necessary for them to know. What Christ said in His lifetime, which they had forgotten, the Holy Spirit enabled them to remember and guided them into the completion of the truth. So, after His resurrection Christ breathed on them and said unto them, "Receive ye the Holy Spirit" (John 20:22). This is inspiration and fulfills His promise to them. This same thought is emphasized in I John 2:27:

"The anointing which ye received of him abideth in

you, and ye need not that any one teach you; but as his anointing teacheth you concerning all things, and is true, and is no lie, even as it taught you, ye abide in him."

One other passage, a very important one, is I Corinthians 2:6-13:

" We speak wisdom, however, among them that are full grown; yet a wisdom not of this world, nor of the rulers of this world, who are coming to naught: but we speak God's wisdom in a mystery, even the wisdom that hath been hidden, which God foreordained before the worlds unto our glory: which none of the rulers of the world hath known: for had they known it, they would not have crucified the Lord of glory: but as it is written,

Things which eye saw not, and ear heard not,
And which entered not into the heart of man,
Whatsoever things God prepared for them that
   love him.

But unto us God revealed them through the Spirit: for the Spirit searcheth all things, yea, the deep things of God. For who among men knoweth the things of a man, save the spirit of the man, which is in him? even so the things of God none knoweth, save the Spirit of God. But we received, not the spirit of the world, but the Spirit which is from God; that we might know the things that were freely given to us of God. Which things also we speak, not in words which man's wisdom teacheth, but which the Spirit teacheth; combining spiritual things with spiritual words."

Here is the promise again clearly stated; that what is to be communicated through this inspiration is something that eye could not see, ear could not hear, nor the heart of man conceive. It is a revelation, and it comes through the Spirit that knoweth the things of God. As your spirit alone can know you (your neighbour does not know you as well as you know yourself), so the Holy Spirit alone knows the will of God, and that Spirit has communicated it to inspired men in man's words. Mark this verbal inspiration: " combining spiritual things with spiritual words."

It has always been a matter of profound surprise to me that anybody should ever question the verbal inspiration of the Bible.

The whole thing had to be written in words. Words are signs of ideas, and if the words are not inspired, then there is no way of getting at anything in connection with inspiration. If I am free to pick up the Bible and read something and say, " That is inspired," then read something else and say, " That is not inspired," and someone else does not agree with me as to which is and which is not inspired, it leaves the whole thing unsettled as to whether any of it is inspired.

What is the object of inspiration? It is to put accurately, in human words, ideas from God. If the words are not inspired, how am I to know how much to reject, and how to find out whether anything is from God? When you hear the silly talk that the Bible " contains " the word of God and is not the word of God, you hear a fool's talk. I don't care if he is a Doctor of Divinity, a President of a University covered with medals from universities of Europe and the United States, it is fool-talk. There can be no inspiration of the book without the inspiration of the words of the book.

Very briefly I have summed up proof of the inspiration of the Old Testament and of the inspiration of the New Testament, and now I will give you some scriptures on both Testaments together. Hebrews 1:1, 2:

" God, having of old time spoken unto the fathers in the prophets by divers portions and in divers manners, hath at the end of these days spoken unto us in his Son."

In old times there were inspired men; but the culmination

or completion is in the Son. That covers both. Hebrews 5:12 also covers both:

" When by reason of the time ye ought to be teachers, ye have need again that someone teach you the rudiments of the first principles of the oracles of God."

Here the New Testament is called " oracles " as well as the Old Testament. Those were Christian people who had learned the first principles of the oracles of God and stopped. Another passage is I Peter 4:11: " If any man speaketh, speaking as it were oracles of God." Peter is here talking about the Old and New Testaments. If a man gets up to speak, let him remember that there is a standard, and that that standard is fixed. He must speak according to the oracles of God. These Scriptures cover both.

Now let us consider some observations:

First, the books of the Bible are not by the will of man. Not one of the books of either the Old or the New Testaments would ever have come into being except by the inspiration of God. I want to give you a searching proof on that, found in I Peter 1:10, 11:

" Concerning which salvation the prophets sought and searched diligently, who prophesied of the grace that should come unto you: searching what time or what manner of time the Spirit of Christ which was in them did point unto, when it testified beforehand the sufferings of Christ, and the glories which should follow them."

Here are men moved by the Spirit of God to record certain things about the future, and they themselves did not understand it. They studied their own prophecies just as we study them. They knew that God had inspired them to say these things, but they did not understand, e. g., God instructed a prophet to say that the Messiah should come forth out of Bethlehem of Judæa. God inspired each and every item concerning the Messiah. To show that these things did not come from the will of man, the man himself could not explain them. It was a matter of study and investigation to find out what these signified. They found out that their prophecies were meant for the future, that is, for us.

The second observation is that the propelling power in the speaking or writing was an impulse from the Holy Spirit. They, the inspired men, became instruments by which the Holy Spirit spoke or wrote. Take, for instance, that declaration in II Samuel 23:2, where David said:

" The Spirit of Jehovah spake by me, and his word was upon my tongue."

In Acts 1:16 we find that the utterances of David were being studied. We have a declaration that the Holy Spirit spake by the mouth of David concerning Judas; and in the third chapter of Acts we have another declaration of the same kind. Always the speaker or writer was an instrument of the Holy Spirit.

The third observation is that this influence of the Holy Spirit guided the men in the selection of material, even where that material came from some other book, even an uninspired book, the Spirit guiding in selecting and omitting material.

From such declarations as John 20:30, 31 and 21:25, we learn that Christ did many things, that if all were written it would make a book as big as the world; that what has been written was written for a certain purpose. The Holy Spirit inspired Matthew, Mark, Luke and John to select from the deeds and words of Jesus that which God wanted written; not to take everything He said, but only that which was necessary to accomplish the purpose.

The fourth observation is that inspiration is absolutely

necessary in order to awaken the power of remembrance. John 2:22 says that after His resurrection they remembered what He had said, that is, the Spirit called it to remembrance.

To illustrate, take the speeches of Christ, viz.: that address delivered at Capernaum on the Bread of Life, the Sermon on the Mount and, particularly, the fourteenth, fifteenth and sixteenth chapters of John.

There were no shorthand reporters in those days, and there is not a man on earth who could, after a lapse of fifty years, recall *verbatim et literatim* what Christ said, and yet John, without a shadow of hesitancy, goes on and gives page after page of what Christ said just after the institution of the Lord's Supper. Inspiration in that case was exercised in awakening the memory so that John could reproduce these great orations of Christ.[1]

Of the orations of Paul, take that speech recorded in Acts 13, an exceedingly remarkable speech, or the one recorded in Acts 26, or the one on Mars' Hill, in chapter 17, one of the most finished productions that the world has ever seen. Inspiration enabled Luke to report exactly what Paul said. Luke never could have done that unassisted. Luke, as a man, might have given the substance, but that is not the substance, it is an elaborate report, the sense depending upon the words used.

The fifth observation is that inspiration was to make additions to the Scriptures until they were completed, in order that the standard may be a perfect treasure, incapable of being added to, unsusceptible of diminution; we want what is there, all that is there, and no more than is there; therefore, when we come to the last book of the Bible, this is said which, in a sense, applies to the whole Bible:

" I testify that every man that heareth the words of the

prophecy of this book, If any man shall add unto them, God shall add unto him the plagues which are written in this book: and if any man shall take away from the words of the book of this prophecy, God shall take away his part from the tree of life, and out of the holy city, which are written in this book."—Rev. 22:18, 19.

It was the design of inspiration to give us a perfect system of revealed truth, whose words are inspired. As an example of verbal inspiration, take Paul's argument, based on the " seed " in the singular number. Everything in the interpretation depends upon the number of that noun. Apart from verbal inspiration, how on earth would Paul hinge an argument on whether a word is singular or plural?

The next observation is that inspiration was to give different views of the same person or thing by different writers, each perfect according to its viewpoint, but incomplete so far as the whole is concerned, all views being necessary in order to complete the view. There is a Gospel by Mark, written for the Romans, beginning with the public ministry of Christ. Then there are the Gospels of Matthew, Luke and John, and a Gospel by Paul. Each of them is perfect according to the plan which the Spirit put in the mind of the writer. They are perfect so far as the viewpoint of each is concerned, but incomplete so far as the whole thing is concerned. We have to put them side by side in order to get a complete view of the life of our Lord. That is what we mean by harmonical study. Each is infallibly correct, but it takes the blended view of all to make the whole thing.

Apart from inspiration, no man on earth can account for Genesis. Just see in what small space there is given the history of the world up to chapter 11—how much is left out. We see the same plan all through the book. It first takes up the wicked descendants, gives their genealogy a little way, then sidetracks them and takes up the true line. Then of their descendants it follows the wicked first a short way and eliminates them and goes back and takes up the true line and elaborates that. That principle goes all through the Bible.

For instance, the first missionary period of Paul's life covered a greater period of time than any other, and there is no record of it, just a single reference to it in Acts. So with his fifth missionary journey. There are only a few references to it in Timothy and Titus. But the intervening three journeys are elaborately given.

Now we come to an important point. When these inspired declarations were written, they were absolutely infallible. Take these Scriptures: John 10:35, " The scripture cannot be broken;" Matthew 5:18, " Till heaven and earth shall pass away, one jot or tittle shall in no wise pass away from the law, till all things be accomplished;" Acts 1:16, " It was needful that the scripture should be fulfilled."

That is one of the most important points in connection with inspiration, viz.: that the inspired word is irrefragable, infallible; that all the powers of the world cannot break one " thus saith the Lord."

Another observation is the power that comes upon the inspired word. Hebrews 4:12:

" For the word of God is living and active, sharper than any two-edged sword, and piercing even to the dividing of soul and spirit, of both joints and marrow, and quick to discern the thoughts and intents of the heart. And there is no creature that is not manifest in his sight: but all things are naked and laid open before the eyes of him with whom we have to do."

Yet another observation is the object of the word. There are two objects. John sets forth the first one when he says that they are written that we might believe, and, believing, have life, or, as Paul says to Timothy, " which are able to make thee wise unto salvation." They are both expressed in the nineteenth Psalm:

" The law of the Lord is perfect, converting the soul; the testimony of the Lord is sure, making wise the simple."

The last observation is on the sufficiency of the word: that the inspired record is complete; that it is all-sufficient. That is presented in two Scriptures, Luke 16:29: Abraham said to the rich man in hell who wanted a special messenger sent to his brothers:

" They have Moses and the prophets, and if they cannot be moved by Moses and the prophets, neither could they be moved even though one from the dead went to them."

The other is II Timothy 3:17:

" That the man of God may be complete, furnished completely unto every good work."

Let me say further that only the original text of the books of the Bible is inspired, not the copy or the translation.[2]

Second, the inspiration of the Bible does not mean that God said and did all that is said and done in the Bible; some of it the devil did and said. Much of it wicked men did and said.

The inspiration means that the record of what is said and done is correct. It does not mean that everything that God did and said is recorded. It does not mean that everything recorded is of equal importance, but every part of it is necessary to the purpose of the record, and no part is unimportant. One part is no more inspired than any other part.

It is perfectly foolish to talk about degrees of inspiration. What Jesus said in the flesh, as we find it in the four Gospels, is no more His word than what the inspired prophet or apostle said.

That is the folly of the Jefferson Bible. He proposes to take out of the four Gospels everything that Jesus said and put it together as a Bible.

What Jesus said after He ascended to heaven, through Paul or any other apostle, is just as much Jesus' word as anything He said in the flesh.

Here are some objections:

First, " only the originals are inspired, and we have only copies." The answer to that is that God would not inspire a book and take no care of the book. His providence has preserved the Bible in a way that no other book has been preserved.

The second objection is, " We are dependent upon scholars to determine what is the real text of the Bible." The answer is that only an infinitesimal part of it is dependent upon scholars for the ascertainment of the true text, and if every bit of that were blotted out it would not destroy *the Holy Scriptures*.

NOTES

1. It is difficult, if not impossible, to interpret this paragraph in any sense other than the obvious—B. H. Carroll believed that the inspiration of Scripture was verbal and inerrant in the autographs, that is, the handwritten copies as they came from the pens of John, Paul, Luke, etc. (Patterson)

2. Once again, Carroll appeals to the autographs. By this he does not mean that translations are useless. He simply intends that copies are infallible only insofar as they faithfully reproduce the text of the original copy. Translations likewise have merit in direct proportion to their discovery and reproduction of the initial manuscript. (Patterson)

II

THE QUESTION OF INSPIRATION RE-OPENED BY HIGHER CRITICS

WITHIN the memory of old men now living, the question of the inspiration of the Scriptures, which had been settled eighteen hundred years, has been re-opened and the agitation on the subject has surpassed anything in the history of religion. Its expressions are found in newspaper and magazine articles and tracts, and for the first time in the history of the subject of the inspiration of the Bible, it has reached the common people. There is not a church in the United States but has members in whose minds the question of inspiration of the Scriptures has been raised. For the first time in the history of the discussion the attack comes from the inside. Heretofore the heathen in their lands and the infidel in Christian countries have been the ones to assail the doctrine of the inspiration of the Scriptures. This time it comes from the pulpit, the religious commentary and the professors in Christian schools. The result has been that distrust upon the subject of the inspiration of the Bible is more widespread just now than it ever has been in the history of the world.

It becomes us to inquire the origin and cause of this re-opening of this question in modern times. It has been a radical mistake to attribute this re-opening and agitation to the progress of modern science. I know that this is what they say—that it is caused by the amazing developments of modern science. Not a word of it is true.

It would be impossible for the question of inspiration to come before science, since science has nothing in the world to do with such a question, and cannot have in the nature of the case. Hence science can have nothing to say about the ultimate origin and destiny of things and beings. It cannot sit as a judge or as a jury upon questions of the supernatural. It can only discuss the natural, not the supernatural. There need never be any apprehension that any matter that touches the supernatural shall ever be challenged to stand before the bar of science and be subject to its verdicts.

While science has not re-opened this question, the disturber is speculative philosophy, which is quite a different thing from science, and there is nothing in speculative philosophy to qualify it to pass judgment in such a matter.

We might ask what has speculative philosophy ever achieved in the realm of the supernatural, where are all questions of Deity and ultimate origin and destiny and inspiration and miracles, in order to justify its assumption to be arbiter of this question? Can any man show that speculative philosophy has ever devised a standard acceptable to any two of its advocates by which matters in the realm of the supernatural might assuredly be known, weighed or measured? Has it ever or can it ever, in the nature of the case, go into an unverified and unverifiable hypothesis with reference to supernatural matters?

Does not the history of human philosophy show that even in accounting for natural things its most assured conclusions at any one period of the world are like shifting sand-dunes in a desert, changing their form and locality with every contrary wind? What it is today it was not yesterday, nor will it be tomorrow.

And if it be so unstable and valueless in the realm of natural things, how can it call for us to lift up our hats to it in the alien realm of the supernatural? How can the finite assume by natural reason to comprehend the infinite? The case is fairly stated thus, by the Apostle Paul in the first chapter of First Corinthians, commencing at verse 19:

" It is written, I will destroy the wisdom of the wise, and the discernment of the discerning will I bring to naught. Where is the wise? Where is the scribe? Where the disputer of this world? Hath not God made foolish the wisdom of the world? For seeing that in the wisdom of God the world through its wisdom knew not God, it was God's good pleasure through the foolishness of the preaching to save them that believe."

In other words, human philosophy, in the nature of the case, can never by searching find out God or things that relate to God and the supernatural.

I declare with all emphasis that if all of the literature of human philosophy on supernatural matters from the time of Jannes and Jambres in Egypt, and the time of Epicurus and Zeno in Athens, down to President Eliot of Harvard and Mrs. Eddy, were put together the whole of it would not be worth the twenty-eighth chapter of Job or, as Dr. Gambrell well says, Burns' little poem, *The Cotter's Saturday Night*.

And I may add that it is not worth one sermon on religion by the Negro preacher, John Jasper, of Richmond. There is less in it than in anything else that ever befogged the human mind.

There are three facts that bear upon the matter of the re-opening of this question of inspiration. The first fact is that before the time of Paul the Grecian philosophers, the Epicureans on the one hand, and the Stoics on the other hand, had attempted to account for the universe and everything in it by a theory of evolution or by fate. That it, on the face of it, left out God and the supernatural, but Paul buried both under his magnificent oration as you will find recorded in the seventeenth chapter of the Acts.

We now come to the second fact. Within the last sixty years Charles Darwin wrote his book, *Descent of Man,* claiming that man is derived from the lower forms of life, and through his coadjutors, Huxley, Tyndall, Haeckel, Wallace and hundreds of others, this theory of evolution was popularized.

It never was popular before, but they so discussed the subject that it reached the people, and it had this merit: it very modestly and quite consistently claimed the position of agnosticism.

In other words, so far as that theory goes, it is impossible to know anything of God, if there be a God. Huxley stated the position when he used the term "agnostic."

My position is that this theory has nothing to do with the supernatural. It commenced below that realm, and so toward all supernatural matters it simply says, "We don't know." Now, that agrees exactly with what Paul says in I Corinthians 2:10:

"God has revealed these things to us through the Spirit; for the Spirit searcheth all things, yea, the deep things of God. . . . But we received, not the spirit of the world, but the spirit which is from God; that *we might know* the things that are freely given to us of God. Which things also we speak, not in words which man's wisdom teacheth, but which the Spirit teacheth; combining spiritual things with spiritual words. Now the natural man receiveth not the things of the Spirit of God: for they are foolishness unto him; and he cannot know them, because they are spiritually judged."

So we see that on this point Paul and Huxley stand on the same platform.

We come now to consider the third fact: Certain school men, coming from Christian schools, began to apply the principles of the atheistic theory of evolution both to human history and to Biblical history with the aim to eliminate all the supernatural. They fell over themselves in the scramble to do that.

These so-called Christian expositors of the Darwinian theory of evolution are hard to describe. They are neither fish nor fowl, neither pig nor puppy. They are like Mr. Lincoln's ox on the fence, unable to go forward or backward, unable to gore the hounds in front or to kick the ones biting him behind, and so they do nothing but bellow.

I say that these so-called Christian exponents of the heathen theory of evolution have driven millions of Protestants back to Romanism, and tens of thousands of others back to atheism.

They have done more to discount the value of Christian schools than all the other agencies in the world put together.

It is a matter of simple fact that a pious country boy is safer on supernatural questions on his religion in the Texas State University than he would be in the great majority of the so-called Christian universities. He is more apt to come back home a sane Christian in his thinking.

These school people who are discussing this subject take themselves too seriously. They are mere doctrinaires, but this much they do accomplish—they create the spirit of irreverence for holy things. A cattleman would understand my characterization of them when I say that they are dry cattle, barren, and unfruitful, and if by chance any of them should give a little milk, it is either blue or too thin to raise cream on, or else it is made bitter by the poisonous weeds that they have eaten, and so unpalatable.

I repeat that the danger from this application of the heathen theory of evolution to the Bible and to Biblical criticism, brings about a new generation of practical men who say, "If there is no such thing as inspiration of the Bible, then we will disregard it. If there be no such thing as God, if the supernatural is eliminated, then we will live as we please."

This is not the schoolman; it is the literary descendants the schoolmen rear. They say, " We will kill, we will apply the torch of conflagration."

Whenever you sow a nation down with the heathen theory as applied to the Bible, you may look for a crop of anarchy —of armed men striking at everything, repeating just what was done in France in the days of the French Revolution.

When this trouble comes; when the practical men put into application what the schoolmen teach, the schoolmen will stand off and say, " We did not mean that; we didn't mean to be devilish like that."

They did not. They were simply trying to exploit themselves, but this crop came from the evolution-seed they sowed.

In Æsop's fable about the trumpeter, you remember the trumpeter was captured, and he asked to be spared; he said he had not fought and killed men. " No," said the other, " but you blew the trumpet and called the men who were armed and who did kill."

I say that a breath of this modern theory is as cold as the last gasp of a dying man, and that what they teach is more fatal to the human race than any fire that fanaticism ever kindled, or any superstition that ever darkened the land.

I will say further, which you will find as you read, that they are in their own esteem wiser than seven men that can render a reason. They believe that wisdom will die with them. They are the most conceited and most gullible and possess the least judicial mind of any set of egotists that ever kicked up a row in this world.

Now, that is what has re-opened this question of inspiration. That is where it came from, and wherever one of them enters a school as a teacher, I don't care who he may be nor what his qualities in other directions, as sure as rain will bring up Johnson grass, he will raise a crop of religious doubters in the school where he teaches.

Now we will take up the question of inspiration, since it has been raised in that way, and in order to get the matter before the reader I will cite the passage upon which I will comment. I will say some things which I have said before, but as this is to be a complete discussion I want every point brought out clearly.

The passage is II Timothy 3:14-16:

" But continue thou in the things which thou hast learned and hast been assured of, knowing of whom thou hast learned them; and that from a child thou hast known the Holy Scriptures, which are able to make thee wise unto salvation through faith which is in Christ Jesus. All scripture is given by inspiration of God, and is profitable for doctrine, for reproof, for correction, for instruction in righteousness: That the man of God may be perfect, thoroughly furnished unto all good works."

I take up first the term, " scriptures." Scriptures may mean any writing, but when we say Holy Scriptures that qualifies the word, discriminating between the sacred Scriptures and all other kinds of scriptures, and when we say, " inspired," that indicates the means by which these Scriptures became holy writings. The inspired writings of God necessarily are holy.

I take up next the word, " Bible." The word, " Bible," is derived from the Greek neuter plural, *ta Biblia*, which means the books—a collection of books. And so when we say, " Holy Bible," we mean the Holy Library.

Now, what books belong to this collection? Everybody knows that they are the thirty-nine books of the Old Testament and the twenty-seven books of the New Testament—sixty-six in all—and in the Philadelphia Confession of Faith every one of these books is mentioned by name, and in the New Hampshire Confession of Faith is this expression, given in the first chapter of this volume and which I here quote again:

" We believe that the Holy Bible was written by men divinely inspired, and is a perfect treasure of heavenly instruction; that it has God for its author, salvation for its end, and truth without any mixture of error for its matter; that it reveals the principles by which God will judge us; and therefore is, and shall remain to the end of the world the true centre of Christian union, and the supreme standard by which all human conduct, creeds and opinions shall be tried."

No man can obtain a position on the teaching force of the Southwestern Baptist Theological Seminary that does not write his name under that article. All the Baptist churches, or nearly all of them in the South, adopt that New Hampshire Confession; our Associations and the Baptist General Convention of Texas do this. That is where we stand on the subject of the inspiration of the Scriptures. And I state as a fact that you cannot find in Texas any reputable presbytery that would lay the hands of ordination on any candidate for the ministry that holds loose views on the subject of the inspiration of the Bible.

Now notice again the words of that Scripture that I cite: The Greek, *ta hiera grammata,* " The Holy Scriptures," spoken of collectively; then it is spoken of distributively, *Pasa graphe.* Every one of these Scriptures is God-inspired. It is impossible for language to be plainer.

Now notice the object of having inspired Scriptures:

That there may be a perfect standard, not an imperfect one—a perfect standard of what man is to be, of what he is to do, of what he is to think, of how he is to live in religious matters; not only a perfect standard which prescribes being, thinking, doing and living, but a standard so perfect that it will convict a man of any departure from that standard, when he has heard it; not only the standard so perfect as to convict, but the standard so perfect as to correct any departure in being, thinking, doing or living.

In the religious realm there are three respects in which the object of inspiration is to furnish the standard.

Now let us notice the next point. It is to make, not only a perfect standard, but a perfect man; that the man of God may be perfect. Not perfect in the sense of sinlessness, but in conduct—well-rounded, symmetrical conduct. John L. Sullivan, I might say, was a perfect man physically, or Voltaire a perfect man mentally, or that George Washington and Robert E. Lee were perfect men all round—physically, intellectually, spiritually, and complete, sound, symmetrical.

The third thing that it is to produce is, not only a perfect standard and a complete man, but a complete equipment for the service of that perfect man. This Scripture says that the man of God should be perfect, completely equipped, as a performer of every good deed. Now, this is why the book is inspired; this is the object of it.

Who is there living that will say Shakespeare is inspired as the Bible is inspired? Could you, from reading Shakespeare, obtain a perfect standard of what a man should think and be and do—a standard that would convict a man of every departure from right being, thinking, doing and living—a standard that would correct every departure from right being, thinking or doing—a standard that would train every one in right being, right doing, and right thinking in a religious sense?

We hear it upon the lips of some people, " Yes, I believe in inspiration; I believe that every writer is inspired."

Well, that is not the kind of inspiration we are talking about.

This brings up the next word. We have discussed " Scriptures," and " Holy Scriptures," and every one of these, *Pasa graphe*. Now I am going to take up the word, " inspiration."

Our English words " inspire " and " inspiration " are derived from the compound Latin words, *inspirare* and *inspiratio*. Literally, those words mean " to breathe on or into " and " a breathing on or into." This is the literal meaning of these words.

Now, what is the Scriptural meaning of these words? We get the Scriptural meaning of the word where God the Father or the Son does the breathing on or into. That is Scriptural inspiration. I have already given a definition of inspiration; now I give a more extended definition:

Inspiration is that communication of supernatural power from God which invariably and adequately and even perfectly accomplishes the end designed by it, whatever that end may be, and which (and this is an important part of the definition) no inherent force that is resident in nature, and no development of, or combination of inherent forces would in any length of time or under any environment bring about.

I want you to get that definition written in letters of fire upon the tablet of your memory: that inspiration, in its Scriptural meaning, is that communication from God of a supernatural power invariably and adequately and perfectly accomplishing the end desired, whatever that end may be. It may be this or it may be that; it is such a supernatural power that no inherent force resident in nature, no development of an inherent force, no combination of inherent forces could, through any length of time bring it about. I will stand or fall on that definition.

I repeat that whatever the need may be—and that means that the needs of inspiration may be various, as I will prove to you before the discussion is concluded—that whatever the need is, inspiration accomplishes that need every time, everywhere, without any instance of failure.

Now we have come to the cream of the matter. We will get at this word by a method that no other man that I know of has ever done. I am going to give some matters that you will not find in any book.

I once delivered twelve lectures on this subject, and I ordered every book I could find on the inspiration of the Scriptures. I have two shelves full of these books at my house, and about six of them are some account; the rest of them are straw. I will take up the examples of inspiration in the next chapter.

III

EXAMPLES OF INSPIRATION EXPLAINED

WE will now take up the examples of inspiration. The best way to test anything is by the usage of the word. The first case of inspiration is in Genesis 2:7:

"And Jehovah God formed man of the dust of the ground and breathed into [that is our word *inspire*] his nostrils the breath of life, and man became a living soul."

What is inspiration? The breathing on or into. What is inspiration in the Scriptural sense? God breathing on or into.

Now let us see what was the object of this inspiration. Here the inspiration of the Almighty not only imparts mere life to the inert body, but communicates an immortal soul, making the man dual in nature, body and soul, and thereby differentiating him from the animals that perish by a chasm infinite and impassable.

The speculative philosophy which I discussed in the previous chapter attributes man to an evolution from lower forms of life, not mere monkeys, but even back to jelly-fish. It attributes man to an evolution from the lower forms of life. It is an unverified hypothesis, even according to its own advocates. There isn't a case in the world where history could say, " Here is a monkey that has changed to a man." Now, it does look like, as old as this world is, that somebody would have seen a case. Hence it is a theory, an hypothesis, and in the nature of the case it is an unverifiable hypothesis.

Now, to call such a case science is intellectual dishonesty. Science is something you know—something that is demonstrated. It is science to put up a great building; it is science that makes the enormous bridges that span the mightiest rivers; it is science that makes iron ships that float, the airships that fly; this is science. We see this demonstration, but to call such a philosophy as this, science, is simply to tell a bald lie.

Now, what is the only evolution that is proven, demonstrated, that can become science? I will quote it for you; it is just what this Book says; everybody will admit that kind of evolution. Genesis 1:11, 12:

"And God said, Let the earth bring forth grass, the herb yielding seed, and fruit tree yielding fruit after its kind, whose seed is in itself, upon the earth; and it was so."

Notice also verse 24:

"And God said, Let the earth bring forth the living creatures after his kind, cattle and creeping thing, and beast of the earth after his kind; and it was so."

Now, what can you develop, what can you evolve? You can only *evolve* what is previously *involved*. Take the acorn, and you have the true story of evolution. It is what is brought out of that acorn. I plant it, and it pushes up through the ground, a little leaf, then a bush, then a tree, and then the tree bears acorns. That is evolution. From the germ of that acorn has been evolved the acorn-bearing tree.

But I venture that if you plant a persimmon seed you cannot from it evolve an orange. Hence the Bible says, " Do men gather figs from thistles? " Each thing after its kind; that is the true doctrine of evolution. It is the only doctrine that is provable. We may put monkeys on a lonely island for ten thousand years, and they will never evolve a man; no lapse of time and no environment will bring it about.

I said that the inspiration of the Almighty, the breathing of God into the nostrils of the body imparted an immortal spirit, making man dual; hence we find in Ecclesiastes 12:6, 7:

" Or ever the silver cord be loosed, or the golden bowl be broken, or the pitcher be broken at the fountain, or the wheel broken at the cistern. Then the dust returns to the earth as it was, and the spirit shall return to God who gave it."

Now, that is the first example of inspiration, where God breathed into the nostrils of Adam's body the breath of life and he became a living soul. To inspire means to breathe on or into. The first case of inspiration in the Bible, then, as we have just learned, was not merely giving life to a dead body, but the imparting of an immortal soul.

Now we take up the second case, which is in Exodus 31:1:

"And Jehovah spake unto Moses, saying, See, I have called by name Bezalel, the son of Uri, the son of Hur, of the tribe of Judah: and I have filled him with the Spirit of God, in wisdom, and in understanding, and in knowledge, and in all manner of workmanship."

Here is a case of inspiration, not as in the first case, in order to impart an immortal soul, but a workman is inspired, filled with the wisdom of inspiration so that in constructing the tabernacle, whether it was a piece of wood that was to be finished, or a brace secured, or a precious jewel to be cut and set—whatever it was, the artificer, through the inspiration of God, was enabled to do the work exactly right. Not approximately right, but precisely right.

Now bear this in mind while I quote the third case, as recorded in I Chronicles 28:19. David is here talking about the plan of the Temple. "All this," said David, " have I been made to understand in writing from the hand of Jehovah, even all the works of this pattern."

Now notice that the inspiration in the case of Bezalel was to enable the artificer to exactly fashion each constituent element that went into the tabernacle. In this particular case David received a plan for the Temple in writing from Jehovah. Every building of any size and beauty is designed by some architect, as Sir Christopher Wren designed Westminster Abbey; as the architect designed the Seminary building; but in this case God's inspiration brought about a document that showed the exact plan of the building that the architect was to erect.

Another Scripture shows the result that this inspiration brought about, viz.: I Kings 6:7:

"And the house, when it was in building, was built of stone made ready at the quarry; and there was neither hammer nor axe nor any tool of iron heard in the house, while it was in building."

Such a thing never occurred before in the history of the world. To be sure, the sound of the hammer and the saw were heard while the building of our Seminary was going on.

Now let us go back to our definition of inspiration: It is a communication of supernatural power by the Holy Spirit so that the end may be accomplished (whatever that end may be), completely and perfectly accomplished, and so accomplished that no force resident in nature or combination of forces in any lapse of time or under any environment could have brought about that result, and so that no human gift of mere genius could have brought it about. There never was an earthly architect that devised so perfect a plan or so executed it that it could be put together without the sound of a hammer or saw; and so perfectly finished a building. As in the case of the plan given, the result intended by the inspiration was perfectly secured—secured in a supernatural manner.

Now we come to the fourth case, and I cite only two verses—Ezekiel 37:9, 10. The case is this: God leads the prophet to look out into a valley full of dry bones, very many and very dry, and God asked the prophet, " Can these dry bones live? " And the prophet said, " Thou knowest, not any way that I know, but thou knowest." And God said to the prophet, in the language that I here cite:

" Then he said to me, Prophesy unto the wind; prophesy, son of man, and say to the wind, Thus saith the Lord God; come from the four winds, O breath, and breathe upon these slain that they may live."

Then follows a description, that as the Spirit breathed on the bones, sinews came on them, and then flesh and cuticle, and then life, and they stood up, a great army. Then God interpreted that vision. The prophet tells what it means.

It means that this valley of the dry bones represents the dispersed Jews, and spiritually they are dry bones, and this breathing on them represents their conversion.

So this case is unlike any one that we have yet considered, and yet it is a plain case of inspiration—that by the Spirit of the Almighty breathing on the spiritually dead soul it is regenerated.

Now consider a moment. No human power could bring about such a result. All the forces of nature resident and potential under any environment or combination can never regenerate a sinner, but the Spirit of the Almighty breathing on a sinner can regenerate him.

That was the puzzle in the mind of Nicodemus, as presented in the third chapter of John. He could not understand. Then Jesus explained that you hear the sound of the wind; you do not see it, and you cannot tell whence it cometh or whither it goeth, and so it is of every one that is born of the Spirit. Now, nobody has ever seen such a thing as that, because it refers to the conversion of the Jews, in one day, as described by Isaiah and discussed by Paul, and that will take place when the fulness of the Gentiles has come. You will see the accumulated force of this argument as we go on with this discussion.

The kind of inspiration we are talking about is the inspiration of the Scriptures; that whatever may be the various ends He has in view by inspiration (and they are various), in every case the inspiration is supernatural, superhuman power, and the result of it is perfect and absolutely certain, whether it is giving a soul to Adam or skill to Bezalel, or the written plan of the Temple to David, to the building of the Temple or to the brooding of the Omniscient Spirit over the dispersed world in one day, bringing all Israel to the knowledge of God.

We now take up the fifth case. When God communicated a soul to Adam, that was the first case of inspiration. That soul was upright, in the image of God, perfect, according to Paul in Colossians and Ephesians, in righteousness, knowledge and true holiness. That is the way it started. As a proof of that, he, without being taught by any one, named the animals that passed before him.

In Ephesians 4:13-24, we have the new man of righteousness and true holiness. Christ's image is formed in him, the hope of glory.

So, then, this case of inspiration is the counterpart of the old man of the first case of inspiration. It is the imparting of a soul imbued with righteousness and true holiness.

Now, approaching nearer to our subject, we come to the

sixth case of inspiration. I quote this case from the twentieth chapter of John, commencing at verse 21:

" Jesus said unto them [this is after His resurrection and spoken to His apostles], Peace be unto you: as the Father hath sent me, even so send I you. And when he had said this, he breathed on them [there is our word, *inspiration;* He inspired them], and said, Receive ye the Holy Spirit."

Now, as a result of that, " Whosesoever sins ye remit, they are remitted unto them: and whosesoever sins ye retain, they are retained." This is an inspiration that brings joy. " You shall do just as I did when the Father sent me; you shall authorize, declare the terms of the remission of sin. There will be no doubt about it." When the inspired apostle told a man what was necessary for the remission of sins, it was the same as if God had told him.

Now, this is a case of New Testament inspiration. God so inspired them that they became mouthpieces for Him, so that He spoke through them, and this kind of inspiration was the inspiration of all the prophets of the Old Testament, as I now want to prove to you from Exodus 4:12. This is illustrating how the inspiration that Christ gave to His apostles, God is giving to inspire Moses: " Now therefore, go, and I will be with thy mouth and teach thee what thou shalt say."

Later we will have something more to say about verbal inspiration. God certainly gave Moses verbal inspiration: " I will be with thy mouth [that is the speaking part of Moses], and I will teach thee what thou shalt speak."

To illustrate by some other Old Testament examples, I will take II Samuel 23:1, all under this same head. We come to the inspiration of David:

"These are the last words of David.
David the son of Jesse saith,

And the man who was raised up on high saith,
The anointed of the God of Jacob,
And the sweet singer of Israel:
'The Spirit of the Lord spake by me,
And His word was upon my tongue.' "

Notice the bearing of that on verbal inspiration.

In Mark 12, our Lord, referring to this case of David, says, " The Holy Spirit spake by the mouth of David, saying," etc.

Before leaving this point, and by way of illustration, take another Scripture as touching the general subject of inspiration. Commence at the first of the letter to the Hebrews:

" God, having of old time spoken unto the fathers in the prophets by divers portions, and in divers manners, hath at the end of these days spoken unto us by his Son."

Or, as Peter expresses it: " Men spoke from God, being moved by the Holy Spirit."

The case we are speaking of is Christ's breathing on His apostles, which breathing is the inspiration, and that is similar in kind to the inspiration of every Old Testament prophet, or other Old Testament writer. Whether he wrote history, or poetry, or allegory, or proverbs, or foretold future events, the record is the result of the inspiration of the speakers or writers.

You will find in some of these cases of Old Testament inspiration where the devil speaks. A man once said to me, " Do you think the devil's speech is inspired? "

" No, but the prophet's words are inspired."

" Do you think that the sayings of wicked people, which they spoke to God's people, were inspired? "

" No, but the record that God says that they said those things is inspired."

Now we come to the main passage that most nearly

touches our case. The most relevant of all these is that passage, II Timothy 3:15-17, which I discussed in the closing of the last chapter, leading up to my definition of inspiration. Let us see what we have found in it and see how it illustrates my definition.

This makes the seventh case of inspiration. I selected seven, in order to give all the different kinds of inspiration, where the ends are different. One might be inspired to speak and not inspired to write.

Now, this is an unanswerable passage, and I never knew a man that could stand before it. I give you my translation or paraphrase: " From a babe thou hast known the sacred writings." We have shown that writings or scriptures mean any kind of writings, but sacred or Holy Scriptures means writings that are superhuman; that the whole selection is spoken of as *ta hiera grammata*, the Holy Bible; that *ta grammata* is collectively speaking, and *pasa graphe* is distributively speaking. All these words in these writings are God-inspired, God-breathed on.

This is a clean-cut definition that covers every book in the Old Testament, and they had the Old Testament just exactly as we have it now. No man denies that the canon of the Old Testament was as we have it now. The whole collection is holy, and every book of the collection is God-inspired, whether it be Job or Ruth or Chronicles or the Songs of Solomon or Exodus—every one of them is God-inspired.

I also called attention to the object of this inspiration. The design of it is set forth here. I will paraphrase and state that design: " Every one of them is God-inspired and is also profitable for teaching what a man should be and believe and do and think, righteously."

It is to be a perfect standard of instruction. Then it says, " for conviction," that is, it is to be a perfect standard by which any aberration in the matter of right being, right thinking or right doing religiously may be made manifest to the one committing the error.

Then he says that it is profitable for correction—that when a defection has been pointed out through this standard, when the light is held by the side of the standard, and the word or thought or deed or the defect has been demonstrated, then this standard is inspired so as to correct that defection.

Then it goes on further to show that the standard is for instruction which is in righteousness, or training which is in righteousness, from being such as I am, thinking such as I do, saying what I say, and doing what I do to a perfect or mature man in Christ. And I want to know if there is any sure, absolute, correct standard that shall teach me what is right—being right, doing right, talking right, living righteously. These Scriptures are *theopneustos* (inspired of God), that such a standard may be a perfect standard—that the man of God may be perfect.

The object of applying the standard of perfection to the man is to make him perfect that he may be perfectly equipped, with a perfect standard as a perfect man—equipment to do any good work.

Now, let us go back to the definition of inspiration. When God does the in-breathing it communicates supernatural spiritual power that in every case secures, with absolute certainty and infallibility, the result aimed at, without any error and in such a way that no mere genius like Shakespeare, Poe, Shelley, Ovid, Homer or Virgil could have attained.

IV

LUKE'S CASE, AND OTHER IMPORTANT
RELATIVE MATTERS

IN this chapter I call your attention to a case where the word "inspiration," you may say, does not occur, but I take that particular case because it is raised as an objection.

A distinguished lawyer once heard me preach on inspiration, and he came to me with this case:

"I want to know how this squares with what I heard you preach," he said. "Luke 1:1-4 says, 'Forasmuch as many have taken in hand to draw up a narrative concerning those matters which have been fulfilled among us, even as they delivered them unto us, who from the beginning were eye-witnesses and ministers of the word, it seemed good to me also, having traced the course of all things accurately from the first, to write unto thee in order, most excellent Theophilus, that thou mightest know the certainty concerning the things wherein thou wast instructed.' Now," he went on, "evidently, from the face of that, Luke gathered his information just like any other historian—no evident inspiration about it; that he traced out everything from the first."

"Didn't those other writers that Luke tells about try to do the same thing?" I answered. "Then why was it necessary for Luke to write an account? Those other writers didn't make things certain; Luke makes them certain. He says, 'I am going to write you an account that you may know the things are certain.' If he were writing to give a mere history to the world, it would not make things certain. What has become of all the memoirs or histories of Christ? Luke says that a number wrote them. Why have these accounts survived—Matthew, Mark, Luke, John and Paul? "

"Well," replied my interrogator, "I think you are putting too much emphasis on that."

I handed him a Greek concordance (I knew he was a Greek scholar) and a Greek Testament.

"What is the Greek word for 'from the first?'" I asked him.

"'*Anothen*,'" he answered.

"Now," I said, "look through the Greek concordance and tell me what that word means."

"Well," he replied, "in many cases in the Bible it means 'from above.' 'A man must be born,' says Christ— '*anothen*'—born from above."

"Very good," I added. "Now let me read the Greek to you and translate it in this passage of Luke: 'Having been instructed in all things accurately—*anothen*—from above.' Why not translate *anothen* that way here, since you do translate it that way in other cases in the New Testament? A good many scholars deny that *anothen* should be translated 'from above,'" I went on. "I have studied what they say, and it seems to me they make out a poor case of it."

My friend replied that he did not know that that word was there. Now note the object was that Luke was to write to produce absolute certainty. He had heard a good many things on this problem. Luke says, "Having been instructed in all things *from above,* I will write you so you may know the certainty of the things that are believed among us."

This staggered my lawyer.

"Anyway, whether you accept that position or not," I said, " you see the need; that when one goes to write a history of Christ he must write about Christ's boyhood; that, Luke knew nothing about. He learned this from God, who told Moses many things and who told Paul about the Lord's Supper. Paul says, ' Jesus told me Himself.' There is no record of Mary telling Luke, as some believe. How did Luke find out just exactly what Elisabeth, the mother of John the Baptist, said when Mary visited her? How did he find out just exactly what Mary said when she sang the Magnificat? ' Now,' says Luke, ' if you would know the certainty of these things you must know them from above.' " *

" I will give you an uninspired account of Christ's boyhood," I continued, " the work that was palmed off on the world by the Roman Catholics, and I will ask you if it gives you strength. Now, will you please read that and see what a silly and indecent thing it is? Notice the way it deals with delicate subjects. Notice the bald immodesty in this uninspired account. Notice the silliness, and then go down on your knees and ask God to help you never to doubt that the Scriptures are inspired. John said that he didn't write everything that Jesus said and did; that he just wrote enough to superinduce faith, that you might believe.

" Now, I was taught that the best way to reach a safe conclusion is to get a large induction of facts and then let a

---

* With the desire to secure the opinion of Dr. A. T. Robertson, of the Southern Baptist Theological Seminary and perhaps the greatest Greek scholar in America, I submitted to him some pages from this chapter in which the author discusses at some length the critical meaning of the word *anothen* and asked Dr. Robertson to give me his view on Dr. Carroll's interpretation of this Greek word. Replying to my query, he said: " The literal meaning of *anothen* is ' from above,' and the context in Luke's Gospel will make good sense with Dr. Carroll's translation of it."—THE EDITOR.

man try them. Therefore, I have selected several kinds of inspiration where the end was different, and no matter what the end was, the end was certainly accomplished."

Then I asked this lawyer to turn to the account in the book of Numbers which tells of Balaam, who didn't want to say what he said, but he had to speak what the Lord put in his mouth. He didn't want to bless Israel, but God made him say what he didn't want to say.

" I will take a more remarkable case than that," I continued. " Turn to that passage in the New Testament where it is said that the prophets received a communication from the Holy Spirit that they themselves did not understand and that they earnestly inquired the meaning of it, but they wrote it down just like God gave it to them, and they studied their own prophecies just like you study them. That was not human comprehension. Oftentimes the prophets did not know the meaning of what they wrote down. Do you suppose that Isaiah comprehended everything that he wrote about the salvation of the Gentiles? They prophesied about the coming of Christ, and they were very anxious about the time when Christ should come and wanted to get a time definitely fixed."

Now, the next most important question is, what is not inspired? Well, first of all, a version is not inspired. A version is a translation. We have the American Standard Version or translation, the King James Version and the Septuagint Version in Greek. We have the Old Testament in Latin, called the Vulgate, and hundreds of other versions. Into practically every tongue that has been spoken on earth this Book has been translated.

Versions, or translations, are not inspired; if they were, all of them would be just alike; but the original manuscript was inspired.

What else is not inspired? Why, the division into chap-

ters and verses. The Pentateuch comes in just one book.
There are different divisions in it, but it was just one book.
That is why " and," " and " goes on through it, connecting
the books as we now have them. We know just exactly
when it was divided into chapters, and who did it. That is
not inspired.

I will even go beyond that, and say that the copies of
the manuscripts were not inspired, and will go further
than that, and say that we have no original manuscript.
We take the three oldest manuscripts—the Vatican, the
Sinaitic and the Alexandrian. These are the three nearest
to the original copy. There are hundreds and hundreds of
manuscripts.

Well, suppose a man had written on parchment, and after
a while some other man comes along, and he wants some
paper and he hasn't any, and he writes on the vellum—that
is, one thing on top of another; now you have to put a
microscope on it to see the first writing.

It would be interesting here to give the story of the manuscripts; also a story of the text and canon, but I must confine my discussion to the subject of inspiration.

I come, now, to ask a question. Some have gone the
Sunset Route from San Antonio to El Paso, and will remember the Pecos Viaduct, where they crossed on that steel
bridge and it made them dizzy to look down into that
canyon, far, far, below. A young man was the architect of
that bridge—quite a young fellow. If he had made a mistake as to the kind of steel, or in one-eighth of an inch of
a certain piece of material, or the wires had been at fault;
if he had not exercised infinite precaution in the knowledge
of material and the greatest knowledge in putting things
together, then the great trainload of people would have been
precipitated into that river.

What, then, do you think is necessary to make the bridge

that will span the chasm between earth and heaven? Is there any mere human wisdom that could do it? We don't want a probable standard—nor one of such uncertainty, but we want something that is absolutely infallible and irrevocable, and the Bible is called holy because it is that infallible, *theopneustos,* product of the Holy Spirit.

The Bible is the Word of God.

All the Bible is the Word of God.

A great many people say, " I think the Word of God is in the Bible, but I don't believe that all of the Bible is the Word of God; it contains the Word of God, but it is not the Word of God."

My objection to this is that it would require inspiration to tell the spots in it that were inspired. It would call for an inspiration more difficult than the kind that I talk about, in order to turn the pages of the Bible and find out which part is the Word of God.

" Oh," says one man, " I can pick them out." But can you satisfy Mr. B.? He can pick them out, too, but he doesn't agree with you. So, whatever you do when you preach, don't preach a spotted inspiration, or you will have to find an inspired man to find the spots.

In other words, with reference to the Scriptures, inspiration is plenary, which means full and complete, hence my question is, " Do you believe in the plenary inspiration of the Bible? " If the inspiration is complete, it must be plenary.

My next question is this: " Do you believe in plenary verbal inspiration? "

I do, for the simple reason that the words are mere signs of ideas, and I don't know how to get at the idea except through the words. If the words don't tell me, how shall I know? Sometimes the word is a very small one, maybe only one letter or a mere element. The word

with one letter—the smallest letter—shows the inspiration
of the Old Testament. The man that put that there was
inspired.

Take the words of Jesus. He says, " Not one jot or
tittle of that law shall ever fail."

The " jot " is the smallest letter in the Hebrew alphabet
and the " tittle " is a small turn or projection of a Hebrew
letter. He says the heavens may fall, but not one jot or
tittle of that law shall fail. Then He says that the Scriptures cannot be broken.

What is it that cannot be broken? Whatever is written
cannot be broken if it is *theopneustos*. But the word is
not inspired if it is not *theopneustos,* which means God-
breathed, or God-inspired.

Let us take that case that Paul spoke of in the letter to
the Galatians, where it is the number of the word, whether
singular or plural, that determines the argument. Paul
speaks confidently and says:

" Now to Abraham were the promises spoken, and to his
seed. He saith not, And to seeds, as of many; but as of
one, and to thy seed, which is Christ."—Gal. 3:16.

If the words are not inspired, what business had Paul
making an argument on one of the words as singular and
the other plural?

Take this fact: Commence at the first verse in Genesis,
" In the beginning God created the heavens and the earth."
The second verse drops from the universe matter to this
earth. Just in one sentence it drops to one particular part
of the universe; then it goes right on dropping from the
general to the particular until it gets to Christ. It drops
every one of the nations down to one nation—Israel—and
from the ten tribes that were dispersed to one tribe—that
of Judah—and from all the families of Judah to that

family that had David as its ancestor, then on to Christ. That is characteristic of the Old Testament. It goes the other way when we get to Christ, from the particular to the general.

Where do you find that in any other book? Suppose a man finds some bones while having an excavation made for the foundation of a house, and another party finds other bones, and so on until one hundred have been found, and you put these bones together, and they make a perfect skeleton of joint and bone of a perfect animal; they make a correct skeleton of an animal, but the bones must all be there. What does this prove by the fitting of every bone and joint, of each part to the other? This perfect articulation of the parts proves that these bones were all the bones of one animal.

Did that happen of itself? There must have been somebody back of all these bones who had the design in the making of that animal. That would necessarily mean the fitting or corresponding of all these parts. The Bible is just like that. There never was a skeleton so well fitted as the books of the Bible.

There was once a little Irish boy who said to me, " Mister, I have something to show you," and he showed me nine speckled puppies and said, " Mister, would you believe it? I can't spare a one."

That is the way I am about the Bible. I could not spare one of these books of the Bible. If you take out one of the collection, the Bible isn't complete. Each part fits into the other part and is a demonstration of the design and the structure of the whole sacred library.

Now, take Sir Walter Scott. I read twenty-seven of his books in twenty-five days. He is a wizard writer—a writer most marvellous—but his books do not fit into each other that way. Take James Fenimore Cooper's novels. His sea tales don't fit his "Leather-Stocking" tales, nor do his land stories fit his "Leather-Stocking" stories. What is the matter? It is just like a train. A lot of coaches put together must have a head, and so there is the great engine, and when that engine moves that coupling-pin holds these coaches together and the train acts as a unit.

The Bible is as much a unit as that train.

Now I am going to give you the most hyperbolical illustration that you ever read. Spread out a map of America and take the great Mississippi River System. Taking our position at its head and looking toward its mouth, we see the rivers that come in on the left, viz.: the Chippewa, the Wisconsin, the Illinois and the Ohio, with all their branches; then on the right, the Minnesota, the Des Moines, the Missouri, the Arkansas and the Red, with all their branches. Now imagine all these tributaries coming into this great river, from the right and from the left, and that water going down until all these tributaries flow into the Gulf of Mexico. That exactly illustrates the Bible.

Take the case of Charles Haddon Spurgeon. He believed in that Book from cover to cover. He believed that every part of that Book was profitable, and he preached four thousand sermons covering every book in the Bible. You can take one set of those sermons and put them together, and you have a complete commentary on the Bible. He believed it all. He preached sometimes from Job, sometimes from Esther. From anywhere in that Word of God, he would take a text and preach from it, and what was the result?

Never since the days of Paul were so many people converted. What else followed? Homes for old widows, orphanages, colportage, missions went out from that one man's preaching, and all over the wide world those sermons went. A boy had one of the sermons in his hand when they found him, dead. A man was found frozen in the Alps with one of his sermons in his hand. A poor convict had his hand resting upon some precious treasure, and he was shot, and a bullet pierced his hand, and the treasure was one of Spurgeon's sermons.

Who ever heard of any one carrying anything of the higher critics around, anything that they have said on inspiration? I tell you the difference: Their criticisms are like jelly-fish—they have no weight, they have no backbone—no legs to stand on—just jelly-fish.

Then imagine one of Spurgeon's sermons drifting out on the sea and a man picking it up, and when he reads it his soul is convicted.

A Hindu was going, on his hands and knees, to the Ganges, to be purified of his sins, and the poor fellow never got there. They found him dead, and his face was illumined, and in his hand was a passage translated from John's Gospel.

What wind brought that leaf to him with that saving message which delivered his soul from bondage and, while gasping in death, caused him to find that Jesus Christ is the light of the world, the hope of the world, and the Saviour from sin?

Now, if we have not a standard, why say A is right and B wrong? If A is right and B wrong, there must be some law that prescribes the right and proscribes the wrong. If you don't believe anything, don't preach anything. God's man would say, " Because I believe, I have spoken."

Recently, with three hundred people turned away because they could not get into the house, I spoke on the salvation of men. All the Christians of the city had come together, and sinners crowded in. I outlined the sermon, and as I presented it in the words of God, if I ever saw rapt faces it was that crowd that night.

The mayor of the city called on me on the following morning. " Thank God that you came here," he said. " I never heard such a sermon. These people will never get away from it, but if you had come here with criticisms, the people would have scorned you."

V

QUALIFYING FACTS ENABLING US TO LIMIT INSPIRATION AND STATE ITS MEANING

AN orderly discussion of the subject of inspiration would be to follow this method: First, the text of the Scriptures; second, the canon of the Scriptures; third, the historical setting; fourth, inspiration.

This method has been adopted in my class in Baylor University and the Seminary, but in the present discussion I am treating inspiration only, and take for granted everything back of inspiration.

In the preceding chapters we have discussed the inspiration of the New Testament and Old Testament Scriptures, the inspiration of the authors of the various books of the Bible, certain promises in the New Testament, then the fulfilment of those promises, but did not have space to discuss another important item, viz.: certain modifying facts and circumstances which help us to define and to limit inspiration.

There are certain terms in the Bible to which we need at this juncture to make reference.

One is regeneration, that work of the Holy Spirit which makes a sinner a Christian.

Another is sanctification, that work of the Holy Spirit which perfects holiness in the Christian.

Still another is revelation, which has for its author Jesus Christ only. He does the revealing, and it is an unveiling or disclosure of any matter which God wishes to make known to man.

And illumination is that influence of the Holy Spirit such as you and I may have obtained by prayer, so as to help us understand the revelation.

Now, inspiration is a different thing. Christ reveals, but the Holy Spirit inspires, so inspiration is that influence of the Spirit (here I carry forward the definition given before) which qualifies its subject to receive a revelation, or to speak or write what God wills, so as to secure the infallible accuracy of the inspired declaration or record. This is a condensed definition of the one which I gave in former chapters.

Now, as bearing upon the definition of the terms " Regeneration," " Sanctification," " Revelation," and " Inspiration," I wish to bring out some modifying facts in connection with the inspiration of the New Testament writers. The first Scripture I cite is John 11:50-52:

" Nor do ye consider that it is expedient for you that one man should die for the people, and that the whole nation perish not (and this spake he not of himself, but being high priest that year he prophesied that Jesus should die for that nation, and not for the nation only, but that also he should gather together into one the children of God that were scattered abroad)," declaring in effect: " If we let him thus alone, the Romans will come and take away our nation."

Now, here is a case of inspiration that will help to distinguish between the terms to which attention has been called.

Caiaphas was a bad man. He was not regenerated, he was not sanctified, but there was an influence of the Spirit resting upon him that caused him to say just what he said, and yet he did not mean it that way at all.

He had an entirely different meaning in his mind. He meant that, as a matter of political expediency, it was better, whether Christ was righteous or unrighteous, guilty or not guilty—it was better for that man to be put to death than that the Romans should come and take away their nation. That was all it was to him. He was the unconscious subject of the inspiration of God; so if anybody objects to Peter's exhibiting faults after he was inspired, it may be replied that the object of inspiration was not to regenerate or sanctify. Here was a man (Caiaphas) who had never possessed that at all.

I take a second case illustrating the same thing. It was customary, when men were crucified, to write the indictment or accusation over the head of the man who was publicly put to death, and so Pilate wrote in three languages—Greek, Latin and Hebrew—the accusation, " Jesus of Nazareth, the King of the Jews," or, as abbreviated by one of the writers, " This is Jesus, the King of the Jews," or, as abbreviated by another, " This is the King of the Jews," or, as still more abbreviated by a fourth, " The King of the Jews."

Now, he wrote that in three languages, and the Jews came to him and said: " Write not that He is King, but that He said He was King." Pilate said, " What I have written, I have written."

Now, the circumstances show that, without Pilate's meaning to, without his having a consciousness at all that there was an influence of the Spirit of God guiding him to write that sentence—writing it in the three languages of the world—it went abroad to the whole human race.

Many a man, without knowing it, has been moved to do things by the Spirit of God. Judas was an inspired man, and is in hell today. Saul, the King of Israel, was inspired at one time in his life. So we must not confound inspiration with either regeneration, or sanctification, or revelation.

Now we come to the second point. Turn to the second chapter of the Acts of the Apostles. I want you to see the particular working of the Holy Spirit that I am going to introduce now. Not only inspiration, but many other powers of the Spirit came upon the disciples. We have this account:

"And they were all filled with the Holy Spirit, and began to speak with other tongues, as the Spirit gave them utterance. And there were dwelling at Jerusalem Jews, devout men, out of every nation under heaven. Now when this was noised abroad, the multitude came together, and were confounded, because that every man heard them speak in his own language. And they were all amazed and marvelled, saying one to another, Behold, are not all these which speak Galilæans? And how hear we every man in our own tongue, wherein we were born?"

Now compare that with I Corinthians 14:27, 28, and you have a phenomenon:

"If any man speak in an unknown tongue, let it be by two, or at the most by three, and that by course; and let one interpret. But if there be no interpreter, let him keep silence in the church: and let him speak to himself and to God."

Now here was an inspiration that came upon those men that enabled them to speak the words of God in a language that they did not know themselves. Some, it seems, had the gift of interpretation.

I want you to see the bearing of this upon verbal inspiration. If a man himself thoroughly understood the tongue that he was going to speak in—if he knew what the words meant—one might claim for him the inspiration of ideas, but not of words. But these men did not know, certainly not in the case of I Corinthians 14:27, 28.

Let us now suppose a case. It is the day of Pentecost, and one of the inspired people is standing up to speak to the people of other nations, and to speak it in their language, although he does not know the language himself. In answer to the question from some Greek in the audience:

"How must I pray?" he answers in Greek, *ho Theos, hilasthēti moi tō hamartōlō* (God be merciful to me, the sinner). But, as a proof that it was verbal inspiration, he did not know what it meant.

Or, suppose it was a Roman, and he replies to that question in Latin, *Deus, propitius esto mihi peccatori* (God be merciful to me, the sinner).

Or, suppose a question in the first instance was in Greek, "What must I do to be saved?" and he answers in Greek, *Pisteuson epi ton Kurion Iesoun Christon kai sōthēsē su* (Believe on the Lord Jesus Christ, and thou shalt be saved), or to the Roman in the Latin, *Crede in Dominum Iesum Christum et salvus esis tu* (Believe on the Lord Jesus Christ, and thou shalt be saved).

I am elucidating this to show the bearing of a certain fact of this kind upon the inspiration of the words. Here it was bound to be an inspiration that furnished the word as well as the idea, because the man is speaking in a tongue that he doesn't know.

Take another case: In the promise of the inspiration which is found in John 14:26, one effect was that it would bring all things to remembrance, and yet we find Paul, in I Corinthians 1:16, saying:

"And I baptized also the household of Stephanas: besides I know not whether I baptized any other."

Now, here is a lapse of memory in Paul, but the question is: Is it a lapse of memory on the point upon which he was inspired? The promise was to bring to remembrance all things whatsoever Christ had said or commanded. Inspiration on one thing doesn't guarantee a perfect memory in other things; it did not bring back to memory the number of people he had baptized.

Let us take another case. It is very important indeed, and I shall have to find myself differing from a great many people in the interpretation of I Corinthians 2:12, 13:

" Now we have received, not the spirit of the world, but the spirit which is of God: that we might know the things that are freely given to us of God. Which things also we speak, not in the words which man's wisdom teacheth, but which the Holy Spirit teacheth; comparing spiritual things with spiritual words."

In this we have both revelation and inspiration conjoined. Here is revelation, illumination and inspiration all together. There are three significant Greek words here, *pneumatikoiō, pneumatika* and *sugkrinontes*, " joining spiritual things to spiritual words."

Look again at the passage before us: " We have received spiritual things, and we have received them not in the wisdom that man teaches, but in the words that the Spirit teaches, joining spiritual things to spiritual words."

That is a good translation of this passage, and is considered so by some good scholars. I cite an authority on that translation, Dr. Hodge, of Princeton, who is as fine a scholar as can be found. He says that this inspiration which Paul received enabled him to set spiritual things, not in words that man's wisdom taught, but in words that the Spirit taught to him which we call joining spiritual things to spiritual words.

It is claimed that *logos* there might mean " discussion."

Now, this has a direct bearing upon the subject of verbal

inspiration, and yet we do not find that verbal inspiration stereotypes the style, even in the case of a single man. It is nothing mechanical like that, nor does it in the least destroy the individuality of the inspired man. When Paul writes, he writes in Paul's style; when Peter writes, he writes in Peter's style.

The Holy Spirit inspires the penman and not the pen, and we must not be disturbed when we find Paul's style, when he is writing spiritual things in spiritual words, or Peter's style in his writings. We should accept that fact as we go along.

In other words, by the wisdom of God, through inspiration, we have a Bible of infinite variety. We have history, law, poetry, parable, allegory, proverb, symbol, simile, argument, persuasion—every form of composition or speech, by all classes of men, and yet each man was moved to speak as he spoke or wrote.

Now let us take II Corinthians 12, where the Apostle Paul is describing how he received a revelation. He had to be inspired to receive it. The inspiration itself qualified him to receive a revelation. John was in the Spirit on the Lord's day when he received the Revelation. Paul is recording a fact that occurred fourteen years before. Fourteen years before he wrote, he was inspired to receive a revelation, and now he is inspired to record it. He says:

" I knew a man in Christ just about fourteen years ago, whether in the body or out of the body I do not know, but I knew such an one caught up to the third heaven into the paradise of God."

So we see that the inspiration doesn't make knowledge perfect on the method, and that is why I don't include in my definition of inspiration, the *method* of inspiration. Though Paul states there the process, he cannot say that he knew so as to state whether it was in the body or out of the body. That is where his knowledge was imperfect.

And then notice that the Bible, both in the New and Old Testaments, tells us a good many things that wicked people said and did, and the question has been asked, " How can that prove the Bible to be the Word of God? " Those wicked people were not inspired of God to say the wicked things they said and do the wicked things they did, but the Book recording them is inspired. Now bear that in mind as bearing upon inspiration.

In the next place, please notice the distinction in the workings of inspiration when the subject of it is writing history, or bearing testimony on the one hand, and on the other hand, making an argument or an appeal.

The most astounding thing in the whole Bible to me is the proof of inspiration on this point. When it comes to writing history, it is arbitrarily given. There are no explanations given. The writer does not stop to go into explanations of the stupendous things he records. Unlike human historians, not one of them makes a solitary explanation. They go on and state the facts arbitrarily, and this is characteristic of both Old Testament and New Testament history.

The next peculiarity is the brevity of its statement. It puts in a phrase what a human historian would put in a volume. It packs into a few sentences the most momentous incidents of time.

Commence with the case of the apostles, and you behold Peter. Peter steps on the stage. Then Paul steps on the stage and he has his say, but they don't stop to explain what the great majority of the disciples said or did or wrote. The history makes no explanation at all.

Then each writer, under his own inspiration, addresses himself to the work before him without the slightest effort to harmonize what he is going to say with any of the other New Testament writers.

Take Matthew, Mark, Luke and John. Matthew commences with Abraham and closes with the resurrection; Mark commences with John the Baptist and closes with the resurrection; Luke commences with Adam and closes with Paul a prisoner at Rome; John begins with Jesus in eternity and closes with his Revelation on Patmos. Paul commences where John does and closes where Jesus Christ turns the kingdom over to the Father. Mark never once stops to consider where the others begin.

These historians go right ahead teaching things in the domain of science, geography, astronomy, history, and going down into all the spheres of technical knowledge. They go right on confronting everything in the wide world, and never expecting to make a mistake in anything, and the man is not living that can show where they ever did make a mistake.

Whether they teach history, science, geography or philosophy, or refer to the weather, the times, the customs, or the seasons, they use the right words or phrases in everything they say.

Take the officer in the Philippian gaol, that Roman gaoler, where there is not a man to witness. It is the most remarkable history that the world has ever seen. They go on and tell us, and it just makes one shiver as he reads.

These New Testament writers voice a statement, for instance, that Christ has raised a young man or a girl from the dead. The young man is given back to his mother, the girl to her parents, and we look to see what the writer says in explanation. He doesn't say a word!

Now contrast that with the feelings and emotions of the personality of the writers when they are not testifying, but

writing letters. Take up Paul's case. We can hear the
very throbbings of his heart. We can look down into the
very depths of his soul. We can hear him say that he
could wish himself accursed for his brethren's sake. We
can see the heaviness of his heart and the tears when he
is writing of his unfaithful brethren, just as you can see
John writing when no man or angel is found who is able
to open the book of future events. Then you see all the
feelings of Jeremiah brought out: " Oh, that my head
were waters, and mine eyes a fountain of tears, that I
might weep day and night for the slain of the daughter
of my people! "

Now that is marvellous. When you go to history, they
are the only people that fail to explain it. They are the
only people that fail to give evidence. Why, you put that
before a lawyer, and he understands it in a moment. They
speak, so that they are the only witnesses that are wanted
on the witness stand.

Now, leaving out things in these histories that you
wonder at, you find that in writing under inspiration Paul
says to Timothy, " Bring my cloak and books at Troas."
I never understood Paul's captivity at Rome until I read
that sentence. In prison!

" I have one old weather-beaten cloak," he writes, " that
I carried with me on many voyages and travels, and the
winter's coming, and I am not able to buy a new cloak.
When you come, bring me that cloak. I am shut up here
in this prison, and I want to read, so bring me the books,
and especially the parchments."

Hereafter let no one talk about that sentence not being
put in there by inspiration.

I now apply some of these facts. Understanding these
things on inspiration, let us go back and apply some of this
to the Old Testament.

I will take up some of the most difficult cases, even worse than that great sea-monster swallowing Jonah. Take II Peter 2:15, 16:

" Which have forsaken the right way, and are gone astray, following the way of Balaam the son of Besor, who loved the wages of unrighteousness, but was rebuked for his iniquity; the dumb ass speaking with man's voice forbad the madness of the prophet."

Now examine what Jude says, verse 11:

" Woe unto them! for they have gone in the way of Cain and ran greedily after the error of Balaam for reward, and perished in the gainsaying of Korah."

Now take what Jesus says, Revelation 2:14:

" But I have a few things against thee, because thou hast there them that hold the doctrine of Balaam, who taught Balak to cast a stumbling-block before the children of Israel, to eat things sacrificed to idols, and to commit fornication."

Now turn to the Old Testament. Notice that it bears distinct testimony to that record in the twenty-second, twenty-third and twenty-fourth chapters of Numbers. There was this man Balak who had sent for Balaam to come and prophesy against the children of Israel. Balaam was rebuked by the dumb ass. Under the influence of the Spirit this dumb ass speaks. The only trouble about the case now is that the uninspired asses sometimes speak. But, speaking seriously, here is a case of the inspiration of an animal.

The most wonderful thing in this world is the influence of the Spirit of God; for He could brood over inorganic matter and give it life; create darkness and light; influence children in the womb; cause a dumb brute to speak in the language of man.

The most alluring quest in the world is the study of the work of the Holy Spirit. Take this case of Balaam, if you want to study the method of inspiration as it relates to the character of the inspired one. Suppose we look a little, first, at Numbers 22:38:

"And Balaam said unto Balak, Lo, I am come unto thee: have I now any power to say anything? the word that God putteth in my mouth, that shall I speak."

Notice again the next chapter, verse 5:

"And the Lord put a word in Balaam's mouth and said, Return unto Balak, and thus thou shalt speak."

And then we have the words that He put in his mouth:

"And how shall I curse whom God hath not cursed? How shall I defy whom God hath not defied? . . . Let me die the death of the righteous, and let my last end be like his! . . . God is not a man that he should lie."

Notice the last verse, where he expresses the vision of the future. Balaam, the man who heard the words of God, prophesied:

" I shall see him, but not now; I shall behold him, but not nigh: there shall come a star out of Jacob, and a sceptre shall rise out of Israel, and shall smite the corners of Moab, and destroy all the children of Sheth."

That is a marvellous prophecy of this wicked man, not a regenerated man, not a sanctified man, but an inspired man, unable to speak for God any word except that which God put in his mouth. God takes this man and inspires him to receive a revelation, inspires him to tell that revelation with infallible accuracy, inspires him to point with an insistent finger into a future so dim and distant that no uninspired eye could see it. A Star! A Star!! And yet wise men shall see that Star at a later day, and find it shining on a Babe wrapped in swaddling clothes, and laying in a manger.

Now let us take two or three epistles. In Romans 15:4, the Apostle Paul makes a statement. We have proven him to be an inspired man. Now he is going to make a statement about the whole Old Testament:

" Whatsoever things were written aforetime were written for our learning, that we through patience and comfort of the Scriptures might have hope."

If he is referring only to the faith of Abraham, what about the book of Ruth, that sweet little pastoral gem? Let me tell you. I read that book over again the other day to see if I could get an inspiration; it came over me like a vision, and I felt the Spirit of God. Here is the genealogy of David. Here is the sidelight on the dark period of the Judges. Here is the proof that while many were going astray and were doing wickedly, a family unknown to history, like one of the seven thousand that had not bowed the knee to Baal and, unknown to Elijah, were keeping the commands of God.

" Well now," I said, " I will read Esther." What is there good in the book of Esther? As I looked over the newspapers and saw the Jews in Russia under the iron hand of persecution—driven away from their homes to an awful exile—yet they are not annihilated. Now, here is a little book in the Old Testament that gives us a picture of a people in exile, and persecuted; that compares this people to a burning bush that burns but is never consumed.

"And whatsoever things were written before time were written for our admonition."

Now I turn to I Corinthians 10:6-11. Here the apostle is talking about that long journey through the wilderness, and of it he says:

"Now these things happened unto them by way of en-sample; and they were written for our admonition, upon whom the ends of the ages are come."

We should look back to the start of that marvellous pilgrimage and be admonished of our course.

Now take Romans 3:9. The apostle propounds two terse questions:

"What then? Are we better than they? No, in no wise: for we have before proved both Jews and Gentiles, that they are all under sin."

He bases the biggest argument that was ever made by mortal man upon two words of that fourteenth Psalm from which he quotes—"all" and "none." *All* have gone astray, *none* are righteous, and on that "all" and "none" he makes the predicate of his treatise. Every word has its significance with him, each one a marvellous word. Romans 10:12: "For there is no difference between the Jew and the Greek: for the same Lord over all is rich unto all that call upon him."

How do you know? Well, I base it on one word of the Old Testament—"whosoever." "For whosoever shall call upon the name of the Lord shall be saved."

Paul, in another instance, as I have already shown, bases an argument on the singular instead of the plural of a noun (Gal. 3:16), and Christ based His argument on the smallest letter in the Hebrew alphabet, and on the stroke of a letter (Matt. 5:18).

VI

DIFFICULTIES MET AND OBJECTIONS
ANSWERED

SOME questions have been raised which I wish to answer. One of these is relative to the scholarly support of my position on the first part of Luke, in which I set forth in a former chapter a possible translation justifiable—a translation that would make Luke claim inspiration for everything he wrote. Those who are familiar with the Greek will understand the explanation better than those who are not. It depends upon the translation of a single word. Luke says that he had perfect understanding of all things, and now comes in the modifying word, " *anothen.*" That word primarily means, " from above." It is so translated in the third chapter of John: " Except a man be born *anothen;*" it is so translated in the letter of James: " The wisdom that cometh *anothen,*" and in an overwhelming majority of cases in the New Testament it has that translation. So that if you translate that word, " Having had perfect understanding of all things from above," it makes his claim to inspiration refer to his entire record.

Now the question is as to whether that translation had any real scholarly support. I stated that John Gill favored that translation, and he was a great scholar of the early English Baptists. But the question now is, " What other scholarship supports it? "

I answer: Matthew Henry, in his *Commentary;* Erasmus, the prince of the Greek scholars; Gomar, another distinguished Greek scholar; Lightfoot, another distinguished exegete—all these men adopt that rendering, together with Galson, the great French scholar, who not only adopts it but makes an elaborate argument in support of it. These are all very distinguished men.

Now the objection made to that translation is, that the verb which accompanies it indicates mental activity in tracing out an examination, and the question arises as to whether that verb is so used. Does the verb require that we should not translate this word " from above "? I will give two uses of the word that are unexceptional, and that bear directly upon the question. What would a Greek say if he were going to use the word *anothen* as it is used here by Luke? What word would he use with it?

Demosthenes' *On the Crown* has a sentence in which we have the same word as used here by Luke. We have the same verb of Luke, and here he wishes to express the precise idea " from the first," and he uses there, not *anothen,* but *ap'arches,* just as it is in the preceding verse, as he wishes to express the idea of " from the beginning." If any one wishes to look this up he can find it in Demosthenes, fifty-fifth line of the First Section.

Another use of the word (the most significant use of the word I know of) is that of Josephus where he institutes a comparison between following sacred revelation on the one hand, and securing information from the people on the other hand, and when he wishes to convey the idea of getting information from sacred revelation he uses this very word, and puts it over against another word that illustrates the idea of getting information from other people. That is a very remarkable thing.

I will give you another use of the word bearing in the same direction. There was a very noted Greek speaker and writer, and in one of the books he used that same verb which Josephus used. Now it is a little singular that we should have this much of Greek testimony bearing upon this point.

Another objection to that translation was that it was not necessary for God to give Luke *from above* a revelation of those things that could have been obtained from earthly sources. I answer that Paul could have obtained from Peter or John (who were still living) all he did not know, yet he did not get a jot from them. God revealed it to him direct.

Then take another point: Balaam prophesied in the camp of Balak. There was not a Jew there to hear it. Moses was not there, but he got a remarkable series of prophecies of Balaam in the camp of Balak. The record of what he prophesied, in the very words, was given by Moses. How did Moses get it? There was evidently a revelation made to Moses of just what Balaam said.

Now still another point: The word in this passage in Luke expresses the highest possible degree of certainty: "That thou mayest know with absolute certainty, the things which thou hast been taught," and that certainty cannot be obtained from the many histories that have been written without inspiration, for he says that many have undertaken for themselves to write these things of what the Lord did and said, "but," he states, "I, having obtained information of all things *from above*, write unto thee in order that thou mayest know with certainty the things which thou hast believed." Certainly, no one needs to be ashamed to stand with such scholars as I have mentioned. It may not be the right translation, but certainly a strong crowd stands there.

I now take up the second question submitted to me. "Please make a little distinction between ' inspired men ' and ' inspired books.'" I answer that an inspired man can only reach his hearers; an inspired book can reach every generation of the world.

In the next place, inspiration did not necessarily accompany an inspired man all the time. It came according to the sovereign disposition of the Spirit.

Balaam did not have inspiration resting upon him all the time. The word of God came to him; God put words in his mouth. When that inspired hour passed, he spoke like other men.

But a book is inspired all the time. The Word of God—the written Word of God—liveth and abideth forever.

Yet again, it would amount to very little to you and to me that certain men nineteen hundred years ago or three thousand years ago were inspired. When they spoke, you did not hear them, and I did not hear them. The need of the inspiration of the Book is to transmit to all mankind exactly what the inspired men said. Therefore, the principle of the inspiration with which we are concerned has to do, not with the inspiration of men, but to make certain the *writing* God inspired, and so far as you and I are concerned it does not make any difference whether the number of inspired men back yonder was many or few. The inspiration that interests us and comes home to us is the inspiration of the *record* that we have.

Now let us see whether the New Testament discusses inspiration that way. Let the reader turn to Romans 16:26. We read it in the English, but it would be better to read it in the Greek.

I want to show that it is not so much the prophets that Paul is speaking about as the recorded prophecy. He is saying that it is not made manifest by the *sayings* of the prophets, but by the prophetic *writings*. The Greek expres-

sion is *graphōn prophetikōn, i. e.,* " the prophetic *writings* "
or " the *writings* of the prophets."

To show again that when Peter used that remarkable
language in his second letter, first chapter, verses 20, 21,
about men speaking who were moved by the Holy Spirit,
he is not discussing the speech of these prophets, but he
uses this language: " We have also a more sure word of
prophecy,"—the prophecy of the *record*—the prophecy of
the *writing*. What Peter is saying is, " Here you have
a *writing,* a Book, and that Book tells you about the
mysteries of God." He says this is the prophecy, or
the writing, that was moved by the Holy Spirit that
took possession of the men. It is the Book that we are
concerned about.

Let me bring the matter still more closely to your
attention. Romans 1:2: " Which he had promised before
by his prophets in the holy scriptures." He did not
refer to any words of the prophets, except their recorded
words. How are these men to get in touch with what
Isaiah, Jeremiah, Ezekiel, Zechariah and Malachi penned?
Paul says, " Which he had promised before by his prophets in the holy scriptures." So you can see what kind of
inspiration we are after. We are after the inspiration of
a Book and not that of a man. Let us illustrate. I want
to give you an idea of prophecy. One of the commonest
meanings of the word is what the man writes from God,
no matter whether it is a prediction or not. It is a writing from God, and is what the man wrote because God
put it into his heart to write it. In Exodus 4, where
God wants Moses to represent Him, to go and speak for
Him, and Moses objects upon the score that he is not
eloquent, God says:

" There is your brother, Aaron. Take him and let him
be your prophet, and you be God to him. I will be God

to you, and you shall be my mouth, and Aaron shall be your mouth."

Now, what is a prophet? A prophet is one who speaks for God; that is why we are getting at His utterance. But how do I know that Moses said those things when he went before Pharaoh? How did it get to me? We learn that God commanded Moses to do some writing, and that writing was deposited in the Ark of the Covenant, and that writing gives an account of all these things.

Now, what are the references in the New Testament to that case? Deuteronomy, the book the Lord commanded Moses to write, our Lord Jesus, in the hour of His temptation, quotes from three times, " It is written."

God told Moses to write that, and Moses was God's *mouth* whenever he spoke. But he was God's *penman* when he wrote, and that which the Saviour said was what the man wrote. So when Paul wanted to make a reference to Genesis, one of these books written by Moses, he did not stop to say that Moses said a certain thing about Abraham, but he says in his letter to the Galatians, " The scripture, foreseeing that God would justify the heathen by faith, said to Abraham."

Now those were the words of God, but those words were recorded, and what Paul is going to use now is in the record. He says that the Scriptures foresaw that God was going to justify the heathen by faith: " In thy seed shall all the nations of the earth be blessed." And now he is talking about those very things about which Moses was commanded to write.

Take the case of Pharaoh. Paul says, " Therefore, the scripture said to Pharaoh, For this purpose have I raised thee up." The thing that with him is inspired is that record which he has in his hand. He is too far removed from that period in time, and too far in distance to know anything about the voice or to hear that voice, but he has that record, and he quotes it in that way: " The scripture says to Pharaoh."

Again: in one of His discussions where He wants to bring out the inspiration of David's word, God quotes the one hundred and tenth Psalm: " Jehovah saith unto my Lord, Sit thou at my right hand, until I make thine enemies thy footstool." Jesus says to these Pharisees, " How is it that David in the Spirit used that lang·vage? " referring to the record.

Then let us see how Peter used it. He takes another one of the Psalms, and he does not discuss the inspiration of David as a man, but he is discussing the inspiration of the record, and he says, " This scripture must needs be fulfilled which the Holy Spirit spake before by the mouth of David " (Acts 1:16).

It is quite probable that David himself did not understand the signification of what he wrote in that record, but now, when Peter used it, he did not employ a proof of what it said, but he simply referred to a record that he had in his hand, and said, " This scripture must needs be fulfilled," and it is true with reference to David and Moses.

I have cited only two cases by way of example, but this is equally true with reference to Isaiah, and with every other one of the prophets. I want to show that it is just as true when it refers to some prediction they were making as when it refers to some historical fact.

I introduce Paul on that. Paul says, " Do you not remember how the scriptures tell us of Elijah's intercession? " The prophet Elijah, in history, is recorded as having dealt with God. He is not now recording prophecy, but facts, and Paul states, as an infallible guide on the subject, the Scripture records of that historical transaction, and his intercession about the prophets of Baal, and so on every other point.

The eleventh chapter of Hebrews takes up the events all along, "according to the scripture." The author commences with Abel, enumerating quite a number whose exploits are recorded in the book of Judges, and goes on clear down through the list to Samuel and the prophets, and it is the record that he cites to prove his point.

At this point I consider the next question presented to me: "Please make a little plainer the distinction between illumination and inspiration."

Well, to illustrate the difference: Inspiration is that influence of the Spirit which enables its subject, or constrains its subject, to write what God wants to be written. Illumination is that influence of the Spirit that enables its subject to understand what is written. One may have only inspiration and no illumination. The reader will recall that I cited the case of Caiaphas, who, being high priest that year, prophesied, "It is expedient that one man die, etc." The record says, "This he spake not of himself." He did not say that of himself. There was an Influence upon him that put those words in his mouth, and he was totally unconscious of it. He did not know anything about what it meant. Illumination comes from God to enable a student of that inspired statement to understand it.

Take that other passage where Peter refers to the prophets who, under the influence of inspiration, having written certain things, were very much exercised as to the meaning of those things, and they prayed God to enable them to understand them. They prayed God for illumination. God declined to give it to them. To inspire these men to write was to constrain them to use the words that God wanted them to use. Illumination is to be enabled by the Spirit to understand the words which God has constrained the writer to use.

This is so exceedingly important in this discussion that I am going to elaborate it a little more. Illumination is an ordinary grace of the Spirit possessed by every Christian. Inspiration is an extraordinary or miraculous gift of the Spirit. Illumination continues with a Christian; inspiration may be intermittent, even with the inspired man. God may inspire him on one occasion by the miraculous influence of His Spirit, and then divest him of it forever afterward.

There are many instances of that in both Testaments, and Paul distinctly says, " Whether there be tongues they shall cease, whether there be prophecies they shall fail," and as Daniel foretold, " the vision shall cease."

Inspiration, having the definite object to make a complete and accurate record of the words of God, is no longer needed. Just as soon as the canon of the Old Testament Scripture was completed, prophecy ceased for four hundred years; and just as soon as the New Testament record was completed, it ceased again, and no man living can, under the Scriptural interpretation, claim inspiration now for anything that he may write.

The object of faith is not a state of mind of the writer. It is not presented as an object of my faith that Caiaphas was a regenerated man, for he was not; that he was a sanctified man, for he was not; that he understood, for he did not. But the object of my faith is his words that the Spirit of God constrained him to speak. My faith has nothing to do with the understanding or the knowledge of the subject of the inspiration. My faith has nothing to do with the character of the man or the spiritual nature of the one who speaks the inspired word, for it may be Balaam's ass which testifies with the inspired words which God may have wanted spoken.

Yea, it may be a hand attached to no body, that mysteriously comes out on the wall and writes the word of God. What concerns me are the words that are written on the wall; that is the object of faith. It is evident that we get at these words by the *record* of these words. Therefore, said the Apostle Paul, these records are sacred books, or, as he says in the letter to the Romans, they are Holy Scriptures; or, as he says again in the letter to the Romans, they are the oracles of God; or, as Stephen says in his speech, they are the living oracles; or, as Peter says, they are the prophecies of Scripture; or, as Paul says, they are the prophetic writings.

"He that believeth and is baptized shall be saved." Believeth what? The object of man's belief is the Word of God, and hence this entire Book is called the Word of God, or the oracles of God. Now, that is inspiration—the inspiration of a Book.

We see, then, that in nature, and in object, and in duration, and in method, there is a radical difference between illumination and inspiration.

A man's illumination may go up and down. There may be a big measure of it or a little measure of it, a big degree or a little degree. But inspiration is a fixed measure, without any degree whatever. There are no degrees in inspiration.

The prophecies of Balaam were no more inspired than that sentence of I Chronicles 1:1: "Adam, Seth, Enoch." That book is as much inspired as any other. And if Luke is inspired he is as much inspired as Paul. If Mark's book is an inspired book, it is equal in its power to any other book. If the Song of Solomon is inspired, the inspiration is as high in degree as Psalm 45, or 23—"The Lord is my shepherd."

I repeat that there are no degrees in inspiration. And we see how it is that there cannot be any inspiration of a book apart from the words of the book. That is exactly what inspiration is—to write the words of God.

And that record extends, not only to the words, but necessarily to the letters which make each word; yea, it extends to the vowel points, for what would a book of consonants be? [1]

And this idea of inspiration is the old idea of inspiration. It is the New Testament idea of inspiration.

It is the idea of Josephus and the early fathers, and only in modern times has infidelity, bald and blatant, seeking the destruction of religion, like a cuckoo, laid its egg in the nest of people who claim to be Christians, and they have raised that up for a real chicken; hatched it out and raised it for one of God's chickens.

There is not a thought even in all of the modernistic books on inspiration of which I cannot trace the fatherhood to an open and avowed infidel who has made open assaults upon the Christian religion, and it doesn't make a bit of difference to me whether they are college presidents or any other great men of modern times claiming to be preachers, or even bishops. When they pat that little fellow on the head and call him " son," we may be sure it is an adopted child.

I now answer another question that has been propounded to me and runs as follows:

" Is not the Bible merely a human expression of a superhuman revelation? That is, there are certain things in the Bible that are inspired, and certain things with which inspiration is mixed, and certain things in which it is not inspired. Now, does not the human element necessarily bring in imperfection? "

My answer is that I don't care whether the element is

human or mule; if it speaks the words that God puts in the mouth there will be no imperfection in the word, and there is no inspiration without it.

I give a crucial test of that: Whoever takes the position that the Bible is merely a human expression of a superhuman revelation necessarily brings out one of two things, and one or the other of these two things comes like a conqueror: That he either sinks the Divine element below the human or he draws up the human element above the Divine.

I give three examples, the first of which is this: There are a vast number of Protestants who hold just exactly that view—prominent men in England, Germany and the United States, Th.D.'s, LL.D.'s, and others having a whole alphabet attached to their names. Mark my point: That position of "part-inspired," "part-mixed," and "part-uninspired"—inspired in spots—necessarily destroys the standard of authority and leaves no standard at all.

Now we will say that a part of the Bible is inspired. I prove it is mixed here, at least the degree of inspiration is mixed—did not need much—and a part is not inspired at all. Who is to determine what is inspired and what is mixed, and what is uninspired?

" I can tell," says one. " I can read the Bible and I can see that some parts of it are not inspired."

Well, then, you are the judge; you are the one to fix what is inspired and what is not inspired. You pass it to B, who says:

" I see the same things, but I don't agree with A."

Then you pass it to C, who says: " I endorse A and B, but I don't agree with them as to the limit or degree of inspiration."

Result: No standard. Where is there an authoritative God's Word under that system? There is none, and there are thousands of young men today that are reading the Bible just that way. They have no standard.

I saw one of them not many months ago. He was reading Paul's letter to the Corinthians, and as he was reading along he was separating in his mind what was inspired and what was not inspired. He said: " Here Paul says he is writing as a man, so that he was not inspired when he said this." Thus he was sifting as he went along. Would that man have any certainties? How long is he going to hold on to inspiration?

I am going to make a test still stronger, and that will bring out more sharply than it has yet been done, the distinction between illumination and inspiration.

The Jews said the Scriptures were inspired, but they had an illumination that put a meaning upon a passage different from the accepted meaning of its words. I quote some of their sayings:

Rabbi Isaac: " Oh, students, pay more attention to the words of the scribes than to the words of the law."

Rabbi Eleazar (and he was on his deathbed when he said that): " Turn away your children from the study of the Bible and place them at the feet of the wise men, whose illumination can interpret them."

Rabbi Jacob: " The words of the scribes are more agreeable to common sense than the words of the prophets."

Let us illustrate by a comment. Jesus said, " But ye do make void the commandments of God with your traditions," a free rendering of which is this: " The commandments of God—that is the standard—but you take away that standard; you make it void and set up a false and shifting standard."

The Roman Catholic says: " Yes, the Bible is inspired, but the Pope and the Council have equal or greater infallibility." Tradition is thus made equal with their Bible, which is a version, a translation, and an exceedingly faulty one at that; that is their inspiration.

Again, they say that the Holy Scriptures do not contain all that is necessary for salvation, and by themselves are not sufficient. I quote their words:

" It does not belong to the people to read the Holy Scriptures. We must receive with the obedience of faith many things not contained in Scripture. It is in the power of the Pope to establish articles of faith."

Our missionary to the Jews writes home a report.

" Here is the trouble," he says. " When I present their own Scriptures to them they have no standard of authority for the Scriptures. They say (quoting a rabbi), ' Scripture is water; the Talmud is wine; the tradition is spiced wine,' and that obtrudes between them and the voice of their own prophets."

Suppose I was contemplating a debate with one of them; it would be impossible.

It has been said that a war between England and Russia would be like a fight between an elephant and a whale. The whale would say to the elephant, " You come out here, and I will drown you." The elephant would reply, " You come upon the land, and I will crush you." One being a land power and the other a naval power, they have no common ground on which to fight.

I cannot have a debate with a Romanist, because we have no common ground on which to stand. I might try to prove my case by the Scriptures, but he would say, " Yes, but the Vulgate says so and so;" or I might quote a Scripture, and he would say, " Yes, but the Pope interprets that thus, and it is the interpretation of the Pope that is infallible, and not the literal Scripture."

Now, how are we going to make an issue? We have nothing by which to decide.

But when we take the Word of God as inspired, whether God causes a dumb ass to speak a part of it; whether God moved a hand that had no arm to write a part of it; whether God influenced Caiaphas, a wicked, vile scoundrel, to speak a part of it; whether God influenced prophets to write a part which they could not understand, the words are inspired, and that constitutes the standard.

Every one of the Scriptures is God-inspired. That is the true doctrine of the inspiration. It is the doctrine set forth in the New Testament.

NOTES

1. Dr. Carroll's persuasion that the vowel pointings in Hebrew words were inspired is not a position advocated by those who affirm the inerrancy and infallibility of the Bible in our present era. Dr. Carroll apparently was not aware that the vowel points were added by the Massoretes around A.D. 500, and hence were not a part of the autographs. However, this passage is not without value since it serves in a unique way to clarify just how thoroughly Carroll, as well as most Baptists of his day, believed in the unadulterated accuracy of the Bible. In light of this avowal by Carroll, those who allege that insistence upon the inerrancy of Scripture is a new thing in Baptist life must once again face the inevitable truth that our forefathers in the faith, almost to the man, believed the Bible to be without error historically, scientifically, philosophically, and theologically. (Patterson)

VII

THE BOOK OF DANIEL: AN OUTSTANDING
EXAMPLE OF INSPIRATION

F OR this chapter we have the selection of a book from
the Old Testament, and a discussion of the inspiration of that book. The book selected is Daniel, the
one about which, in recent years, there has been the most
controversy.

First, I call attention to the fact that the book of
Daniel, from the time it was first written until the time
of Christ, impressed the imagination of the people more
than any other book of the Old Testament, just as the
book of Revelation has impressed the public mind and the
imagination since it was written, more than any other book
of the New Testament.

The circumstances connected with Daniel were very
much like the circumstances of Joseph and Moses. The
reader will recall that Joseph was taken as a prisoner
into a foreign land, and there, on account of his purity
and piety, and the favor of God, he was exalted to the
chief position in the government of that nation, precisely similar to the case of Daniel, who was taken to
Babylon and attained the highest position in the court
there.

Many hundreds of years after Joseph came Moses, and
Moses also was exalted to the highest position in the foreign government where his people were in bondage, and
he was learned in all the wisdom of the Egyptians, and

the favor of God was upon him. The circumstances of Daniel were very much like the circumstances which surrounded Moses.

The book of Daniel is written in two languages. From the fourth verse of the second chapter to the end of the seventh chapter is written in Aramaic. The first chapter and three verses of the second chapter, and from the eighth on, it is written in Hebrew. The transition from Hebrew to Aramaic is very remarkable, and the transition back to Hebrew is equally remarkable.

The circumstances under which the transition takes place sufficiently explains the transition to any thoughtful mind. I shall not discuss that phase of the subject here. I simply call attention to the fact.

The Hebrew part of it is about like the Hebrew of the contemporaries of Daniel, and the Aramaic is about like the Aramaic of the contemporaries of Daniel. Such is the testimony of the best scholarship upon this point.

Now, the reason I have chosen Daniel to illustrate the inspiration of a Book is that its inspiration has been attacked upon the following grounds:

First, they say that it had no place in the Jewish canon of Scripture; that it was a novel written by a gifted Jew, say about one hundred and fifty years before Christ, in the time of the Maccabees.

Then they allege that the book cannot be inspired, because of false historical statements made in it. They deny the statement in the beginning of the book that there was any deportation of the Jewish people in the third year of the reign of Jehoiachim to Babylon. They say that is a false statement. They deny, as a matter of fact, that there was any Belshazzar, king of Babylon. They deny that Babylon was taken as represented in the book of Daniel. These are some among the matters of fact which they deny, and therefore they question its inspiration.

They then question its inspiration on account of the "incredible" miracles which it relates, and the "incredible" predictions which it makes. They admit that a large part of the predictive portions of the book exactly correspond to the age of Antiochus Epiphanes, but they claim the book was written after these events.

Now they claim that these are the grounds upon which the book of Daniel has been denied a place among the books of God. It is these objections that I wish to answer, and the first point that I make, or the first question I ask, is this: Was the canon of the Old Testament completed before the Maccabean period? Were all the books of the Old Testament written, as we now have them, before the time of Judas Maccabæus? His history is set forth in the Apocryphal book of Ecclesiasticus, a very fine book, though not inspired, and a book well worth reading. It is conceded that this book was written two hundred years before Christ. The grandson of the man who wrote it translated it into Greek one hundred and thirty years before Christ, and issued a preface, and now I quote from that preface. This book can be found in any of the large Bibles which contain also the Apocryphal books. He says:

"My grandfather, seeing that he had much given himself to the reading of the law, of the prophets, and of the other books of the fathers, and had gotten therein sufficient learning, was drawn himself to write something pertaining to learning and wisdom."

That is only a part of the preface, but the reader will note that the preface states the three divisions of the Old Testament—the law, the prophets and the other books, or writings—and three times he makes that statement in the preface—that the author of Ecclesiasticus, who wrote the book two hundred years before Christ, had, before he wrote his book, given much attention to the reading of this three-fold division of the Old Testament—the law, the prophets, and the other writings.

Nobody has ever been able to question the accuracy of the statement by this historian. We do not accept him as an inspired writer, but we do accept him as a competent historian who states a fact. This can be found now in any Jewish Bible just as he quotes it; so it appears in the Jewish Old Testament today, which, with the exception of the Apocrypha, is exactly like our Old Testament. The order of the books is not the same, but all the books are there, and they are just the same as our Old Testament.

The next historical fact that I cite is the prevalent Jewish tradition which nobody questions, that the Old Testament canon was completed in the days of Ezra and Nehemiah, and that the last book added was the book of Malachi. That tradition can be found in writing in a number of places, and I could quote a great many passages in the Old Testament that make it extremely probable that this is correct, but I merely wish to cite historical facts. It is therefore a settled Jewish tradition that the canon of the Old Testament was closed in the days of Ezra and Nehemiah, who were contemporaries of Daniel.

The third historical fact is the testimony of Josephus, who himself cites this Jewish tradition, and who goes on to state that no book could possibly have been added after the days of Ezra and Nehemiah, because no Jew would accept, in his canon of Scripture, a book that had not been given by a prophet or approved by a prophet.

He says that after that time prophecy ceased in Israel, and that while they had a great many books written after that time, they were not accepted as inspired books. So here are three historical testimonies.

My next question is, Was the book of Daniel in that list? If the book of Daniel was in the list of the Jewish sacred books as part of the law or the prophets, or other writings, that settles its inspiration and thoroughly answers at least two of the objections made against the book.

Without citing a vast multitude of authorities, I give a single statement by Eidersheim, one of the greatest of the Hebrew scholars. In the second volume of his *Life of Christ,* and in the fifth appendix, he pays a great deal of attention to the formation of the Jewish canon and the books that enter into that canon, and says: " No Jew of the ancient synagogue ever questioned the right of Daniel's place in the canon of the Old Testament Scriptures," and he challenges the world to show a single instance.

In Smith's *Bible Dictionary* is an article on the book of Daniel by Westcott, one of our greatest Hebraists, and he states about the same thing that Eidersheim does with reference to it.

Let us now examine the testimony of Josephus upon Daniel. He not only places Daniel among the sacred books, but he refers to some of his remarkable predictions which have been fulfilled and, in closing, he says, " Now, as for myself, I have so described these matters as I have found them and read them; but if any one is inclined to another opinion about them, let him enjoy his different sentiments without any blame from me."

He also says that the prophetic character of the book

of Daniel was by the Jews placed higher than any other book of the Old Testament, except the Law of Moses.

In the next place, nobody denies that the book of Daniel is in the Septuagint translation, the Greek version of the Old Testament. These are historical evidences to show about the canon and about the books being in the canon.

The next question is, " Does any Old Testament book refer to Daniel to show that he was a real person, and that he lived at the time specified in his book, and that his character corresponds to the character set forth in the book? "

The only place that one could find this would be in some book written by a contemporary, and I will cite such a book: Ezekiel was a captive in Babylon at the time Daniel was. He was brought there some time later, but the two were there together. Ezekiel was a prophet to the people of Israel in Babylonian bondage. Daniel was an officer of the court. Now here is Ezekiel's testimony. Ezekiel 14:13, 14:

" Son of man, when the land sinneth against me by trespassing grievously, then will I stretch out mine hand upon it, and will break the staff of the bread thereof, and will send famine upon it, and will cut off man and beast from it. Though these three men, Noah, Daniel, and Job, were in it, they should deliver but their own souls by their righteousness, saith the Lord God."

Verse 20 of the same chapter reads:

" Though Noah, Daniel and Job were in it, as I live, saith the Lord God, they shall deliver neither son nor daughter; they shall deliver but their own souls by their righteousness."

Another passage from the same book—Ezekiel 28:3—reads:

" Behold, thou art wiser than Daniel: there is no secret that they can hide from thee."

These are the references. In the first and second, a reference is made to the righteousness of Daniel, and in them he is associated with Noah and Job; Noah interceding for the whole world, but able to save none of them, except himself and his family, by his righteousness; Job interceding for his three friends, and Daniel interceding for his people in captivity. The last reference shows the extraordinary wisdom of Daniel.

Now we must either assume that there were two Daniels, one who had lived in the time of Ezekiel, whose piety and intercessory power in prayer and whose wisdom were so remarkable as to make him a colossal figure in the mind of Ezekiel, and that some man far subsequent to this time wrote the book and put it off as a forgery under the name of this Daniel, or that Daniel wrote the book that is attributed to him. But Ezekiel's facts came from the book of Daniel. It is in the book of Daniel that we find out about his piety, his intercession and his righteousness.

In the next place, they say this book was written by a forger in the days of the Maccabees. Now against that I submit two quotations from the book of Maccabees. The first page of the first book of Maccabees, fifty-fourth verse, quotes the following passages from the book of Daniel:

"And from the time that the daily sacrifice shall be taken away, and the abomination that maketh desolate set up, there shall be a thousand, two hundred and ninety days."

When the book of Maccabees was written there was the Daniel literature in the hands of the writer of the book, and he quotes from it; but in the second chapter of the book of Maccabees, fifty-ninth and sixtieth verses, he quotes from the book of Daniel about the three Hebrew children in the fiery furnace, and how that God preserved their lives, and then he quotes that Daniel himself, though innocent, was cast into the den of lions, and was saved by the power of his God.

I cite another fact: The impress of the book upon the inter-Biblical period appears by the number of myths and legends that attach themselves to this book. In the Catholic Bible we find in that chapter that tells about the three Hebrew children in the furnace—right in the midst of that account—a number of verses purporting to give the song of the three Hebrew children —the song they sang while in that fiery furnace. This Apocryphal writer of the inter-Biblical period had the history Daniel wrote about the preservation of these Hebrew children.

Then we find at the end of the book two appendices which the Roman Catholics receive. One is the account of Susanna, and the other, the Dragon. Here are three Apocryphal traditions, or legends, which have fastened themselves upon the book of Daniel, and such is the character attributed to him for wisdom, and his veracity in writing the account of the three Hebrew children that these traditions continue to survive.

But Dr. Farrar objects to the book of Daniel because " it made no impress upon the inter-Biblical period." That is his objection to the book. But here is the history, and here are three legends that, during this period, grew up and attached themselves to the book. They are not in the Hebrew canon, of course, but we find them appended to the book in the Septuagint translation.

The next question is, "What has the New Testament to say about the book of Daniel?" I cite first Matthew 24:14, 15:

"And this gospel of the kingdom shall be preached in all the world for a witness unto all nations; and then shall the end come. When therefore ye see the abomination of desolation, which was spoken of through Daniel the prophet, standing in the holy place (let him that readeth understand)."

Jesus is answering three questions here: When shall the Temple be destroyed? When shall Jerusalem be destroyed? What shall be the sign of His coming and the end of the world? His answer is:

"When therefore ye shall see the abomination of desolation spoken of by Daniel the prophet, flee unto the mountains."

Now, this is the testimony of our Lord Jesus Christ. He quotes from Daniel the prophet. He cites that remarkable prediction of the desolation set forth in the last chapter of Daniel. Now let us look into the next chapter, Matthew 26:64. Here Jesus Christ is again speaking:

"Hereafter shall ye see the Son of man sitting on the right hand of power, and coming in the clouds of heaven."

Where from the Old Testament could such a conception

as that be found? We find it in the seventh chapter of Daniel, where the Son of man comes to the Ancient of Days, and where there is given unto Him a kingdom, and power, and great glory, and that expression, " Son of Man." There is no other book of the Bible from which it could be taken, except the book of Daniel.

Here, also, we find " the Kingdom of Heaven," the institution of the Kingdom represented by the Stone that was seen cut out without hands, and that struck the image that represented the kingdoms of the world and that broke them up in pieces and scattered them. Our Saviour refers to that when telling how His Kingdom shall be preached throughout all the world, and says:

" Whosoever falls upon this stone, he shall be broken, and upon whomsoever this stone shall fall, he shall be ground to powder."

Suppose we look at the miracles recorded in Daniel. In Hebrews 11:33 we find that miracle of preservation from fire quoted by the author of the letter to the Hebrews.

Let us also look at the doctrine of the angels, as set forth in the book of Daniel. In Luke 1:19-26, we see the angel Gabriel appearing to Zacharias and to Mary.

Now let us look at the analogues that Daniel furnishes. We see them reproduced in the book of Revelation, so that the book of Revelation and the book of Daniel stand or fall together. The thirteenth chapter of Revelation and the seventh, eighth and eleventh chapters of Daniel must fall together, or stand together forever.

We now look at Paul's " man of sin " that speaks the great swelling words of blasphemy and thinks himself above God. Unquestionably he gets it from Daniel 7:26, and it is again referred to in Revelation 13:5. It is thus evident that the New Testament certifies to the prophecies of Daniel, the miracles of Daniel, the history of Daniel, and the inspiration of Daniel.

Here, then, we have the Old Testament in Ezekiel, the inter-Biblical period in the book of Maccabees, and the New Testament in Christ and Paul and John, all pointing to this book as a proof of God's revelation and inspiration.

Let us now look at the objections, which are: first, that this book is a forgery; second, that certain statements made in it are falsehoods unsupported by any historical evidence; third, that the miracles in it are incredible; and fourth, that the predictions in it are incredible.

Let us look at the matter of fact. I have examined with great care the statements made in the first chapter of Daniel. He says that Nebuchadnezzar came to Jerusalem in the third year of the Jewish King (Nebuchadnezzar at that time was not King, but Prince Royal) and that he took back with him certain Jewish prisoners of the princes: Daniel and those three young men, specifically mentioned in the book of Daniel, are all identified in the beginning of the book as having been taken by Nebuchadnezzar.

Now what the objectors claim is, that Nebuchadnezzar never made that expedition. The statements made in Jeremiah and in Herodotus, the Greek historian, and in Josephus with reference to this matter, are simply inexplicable unless this fact occurred just as Daniel says it did.

Take the next objection stated. They claim that Daniel's statement about Nebuchadnezzar's madness—that he lost his mind for a number of years and ate grass like an ox—is unsupported, but it is that very fact that the Babylonian historians confirm, and a number of other historians who testify to that very derangement of mind of Nebuchadnezzar.

The next fact is that about Belshazzar. Now, upon what ground do they dispute the capture of Babylon and the death of Belshazzar? They dispute it upon one solitary ground, the recent discovery of a tablet set up by Cyrus to commemorate his conquest of Babylon. Let us assume, in the first place, that this tablet says what they claim it says. But, on the other hand, what is it?

There is first the testimony of Xenophon in his history, who lived there in his time, and whose account of the conquest of Babylon harmonizes with Daniel. Then we put over against it the testimony of Herodotus, the father of history, who lived near that time, and his accounts and the account of Daniel are in harmony.

Here, now, are three historians—Daniel, Xenophon and Herodotus—and the critics propose to offset the testimony of these three historians by a little tablet scarcely discernible. The inscriptions on it—the most important part of them—are defaced or rubbed out, so that one cannot make out what it says. And yet it is a fact that the tablet confirms the Daniel account, according to the best translations of that tablet. It is needless to go over all of this. I simply say that a close examination of the tablet clears up the only point of doubt in it, viz.: as to whether Darius the Mede entered into Babylon. Somebody died that night. The inscriptions read, " the King's son," and the King's son was Belshazzar. Daniel testifies that Belshazzar was to die the very night of the capture of Babylon. That tablet declares that on that very night a certain important personage died, which filled the whole land with mourning.

Now, the question is, How are we going to read it? They say we should read it, " the King's wife." We say that we should read it, " the King's son." While there can be no certainty attached to it, it ought to be the King's son that died, and, giving it this reading, the tablet and the record in Daniel are in harmony; and no matter what the tablet may have said, it is not sufficient to displace the testimony of three competent historians—one, Daniel, living at the time, and one Xenophon, living so near the time and writing upon matters of which he is fully informed, and Herodotus, the father of history. So the historians and the Greek stand together, and the tablet may be harmonized with them.

Now with reference to the miracles: They say that the miracles are incredible, yet any miracle is incredible from a human standpoint. The question is, was there an occasion for special miracles at this juncture? It certainly was a transition period. The Jewish polity had just been destroyed. The people had been led into captivity. They were now passing through one of the most vital transitions in all of their history, and it is always at those periods that miracles are introduced.

Miracles became necessary in the time of Moses to attest him, to accredit him in the movement that led the people out of their captivity and to establish them as a nation in their own country, and the character of the miracle corresponded with the necessity of the case. Here are the people in captivity again. Here is a great man like Joseph and Moses, the man of highest power among his people, and if ever miracles were needed to give credentials to a man through whose mighty influence Israel was to be restored, it was needed now. So, there is nothing incongruous in the miracles of that period.

Suppose we take a passage from the Scriptures on this.

I cite Micah 6:5: " O my people, remember . . . that ye may know the righteous acts of Jehovah." The reference is to the effect that, as in the days of Moses, God intervened with mighty wonders, so He will again intervene under similar conditions. That is the substance of the statement.

The point I am seeking to impress is that miracles in the New Testament time were never introduced unless they were necessary. There must be an occasion to justify them. The conditions justified the kind of miracles that were brought to pass in Daniel's time; and if we object to this book on the basis of miracles, we can object to any other book in the Bible just as well.

Now let us look at the predictions. What is the matter with the predictions? The critics say that the references to the four successive kingdoms, culminating as they did with full explanations about the Greek and Persian kingdoms, were so very exact that they must be history instead of predictions. They make exactly the same objections to the fifty-third chapter of Isaiah. They say that Isaiah's picture of the sufferings of our Saviour is so exact—that it is so precisely fulfilled in the coming of our Lord Jesus Christ—that it must have been written after the coming of Christ.

But let us take another prediction in the book. This prediction, if it had any fulfilment at all, had to be fulfilled after the writing of the book. Here it is:

" Seventy weeks are decreed upon thy people and upon thy holy city, to finish transgression, and to make an end of sins, and to make reconciliation for iniquity, and to bring in everlasting righteousness, and to seal up vision and prophecy, and to anoint the most holy. Know therefore and discern, that from the going forth of the commandment to restore and to build Jerusalem unto the

Anointed One, the prince, shall be seven weeks, and three-score and two weeks:" (that is, sixty-nine weeks,) " and it shall be built again, with street and moat, even in troublous times. And after the threescore and two weeks shall the Anointed One be cut off, and shall have nothing: and the people of the prince that shall come shall destroy the city and the sanctuary; and the end thereof shall be with a flood, and even unto the end shall be war; desolations are determined."

Here is a prediction that, first of all, points to the destruction of Jerusalem. The city is to be destroyed; next, the vision and the oblation are to cease, so there are to be no more offerings upon the Jewish altar; next, to make reconciliation for sin; next, the coming of Messiah, the Prince; then the cutting off of the Messiah to be followed by the destruction of the city and the sanctuary. That is the prediction, and the time is given, and that is one of their objections to it—the specific time given.

Now I submit one simple test, set forth over and over in the prophecies. Sixty-nine weeks must pass before Messiah comes. The Jewish method of computation at that time was to count thirty days to the month, and just exactly to a day from the issuing of the decree to rebuild Jerusalem, as we find in the second chapter of Nehemiah —just to a day from the issuing of that decree, sixty-nine weeks of years, Jesus of Nazareth came into Jerusalem, and the multitudes spread their garments before Him and quoted the words of the prophet Zechariah about the coming of the Kingdom and the Messiah of the Kingdom, who was Jesus of Nazareth. In other words, the crucifixion of Christ under the statement that I have just made, fits the prophecy of Daniel, not to a year, not to a month, but to a day; and if the Messiah-Prince has not come, when is He to come? He was to come before Jerusalem was destroyed.

We know that it is the doctrine of our belief as much as we believe anything about the Bible, that when He died He made reconciliation for sin, and that it was then that He brought in everlasting righteousness; and we do know that after the destruction of Jerusalem the oblation ceased; and we do know that the vision has closed, that prophecy has ceased. Now, that is the prediction. I know of nothing in all the prophecies of the Bible so remarkable as that ninth chapter of Daniel. Now they claim that the book was written as late as one hundred and fifty years before Christ!

This is one of its predictions. Let us now take another—the prediction that those kingdoms of this world are to be given over to the saints of the Most High God—and compare this with the prophecy of Jesus in the twenty-fourth and twenty-fifth chapters of Matthew, also the prophecy of Jesus in the book of Revelation, and if one can deny the inspiration of Daniel he must deny the inspiration of Christ. If he can take away the authority of that book he may take away the authority of any book in the Bible.

I don't know any better exemplification of the folly of the higher critics than the issue that they have made upon the book of Daniel. I don't know of one single point that they can sustain as a matter of fact in history. Suppose, for example, to illustrate their questionings of the integrity of this book, this argument: " There are certain Greek words in the book that demand a later day for its writing than the date assigned to it."

The first time that I saw that argument I thought it must be something very formidable. What are those Greek words? They are just two—the names of two instruments of music. Two Greek instruments of music are referred to under their Greek names, and that, they say, demands a later date for the book than the time assigned to it.

Let us go back to the time assigned to it, and that is about the time of Ezekiel and Jeremiah. Was there any contact with the Greek world up to that time? Had there been any touch with the people of Greece that would at least account for the names of two musical instruments in the book?

No other fact of history is established more clearly than that. The only mystery to me is that there are not more such words, and how puerile that sounds to make such a tremendous assertion upon such a trivial basis as that!

The subject for the next chapter is this: Why have inspired books, and especially inspired in their words, unless we have the precise text of the books?

Second: Why have inspiration of words when the masses of the people have to depend upon translations and versions, as we do?

Now, as the words, as originally given, are lost, and we depend upon copies only, and as we admit that the copies vary, and that we have to depend upon the translations of those copies, then why insist upon inspiration?

These are two of the objections that will be answered in the next chapter, with some others of like nature.

VIII

SOME QUESTIONS ANSWERED AND A RÉSUMÉ OF THE WHOLE DISCUSSION OF INSPIRATION

THIS closing chapter will be devoted to a very brief review of the general subject, so as to fix in the mind what we have discussed. Before doing that, however, I answer some questions propounded oftentimes, to this effect:

The theory of verbal inspiration is objected to on the ground that it means merely the inspiration of the autographs—the original manuscripts—and that none of the original manuscripts survive. In fact, there is no autograph copy of any ancient book of the Bible, "and the copies that we have," says this objector, "are so varied as to the text that it is practically impossible to assume verbal inspiration."

They further state that the great variety of the texts of the New Testament books alone show at least fifteen hundred variations in the text. This was discovered after the first Bible was printed, when they began to print the Bible, so that all the copies were necessarily exactly alike. The impress from the types would be exactly the same, and it was no longer possible for variations of the text to occur, so that the variation of texts lies a thousand years back of 1456, the time of the printing of the first Bible. Within this period of a thousand years we were dependent upon copies of the New Testament, and there were multitudes of these copies, and the variations amount to, say, fifteen hundred.

My reply to that is, in the first place, that if every variation claimed was granted, it in no way interferes with any doctrine or promise or duty commanded in the Bible.

In the next place, when you take out the variations they amount to nothing; that is to say, they are the mere transposition of words, or some constructions of grammar that in no way materially affect the sense. When you take out those variations only about one one-thousandth part of the New Testament is affected by the variations— one part out of a thousand—and out of that thousandth part the only variations that might change anything can be counted on the fingers. So that when it is carefully scrutinized this whole question of the variations of the text is a very weak argument.

The first reason is that no other books in the world in their copies show so little variation. Other books since printing was introduced show more variations than the variations of the New Testament.

We have more copies and more harmonious copies of the New Testament than of any other book in the world. The copies of the New Testament books were carefully prepared.

In the next place, it has not been deemed essential to go back to the original of any other book with anything like the degree of zeal and energy that has been manifested in getting back to the original of the Bible. The work of scholars, the journeys taken, the expense incurred, the years of toil which they have devoted to the subject, and a great multitude of them of all enlightened nations, show that there is an importance in getting at just what the Holy Spirit says in the matter of the New

Testament books that does not apply to any other book in the world. We hear of nothing like that on the Koran or the Book of Mormon.

Now if we can count on our fingers all the important variations in the text of the New Testament, that fact, instead of being against verbal inspiration, is in favor of verbal inspiration.

The second question propounded was this: "Is there any need of verbal inspiration, since the masses of the people have to rely upon a translation anyhow? Not many people read the Hebrew and the Greek texts, but most of them have to read in their native tongue. Inasmuch as the people have to depend upon translations, why make such a to-do about the inspiration of the original?"

The first time I ever did any carpentering I wanted to put up a small fence, and I thought I could do the work myself. I thought it was useless to hire a carpenter to put up a little picket fence. There were some pieces of timber that had to be sawed in equal lengths and then nailed up, and I thought I could do that as well as anybody, and so I measured off my first paling the height I wanted it, and measured my second one by that. Then I laid aside the first one and measured the third paling by the second, the fourth by the third, the fifth by the fourth, and so on, and by the time I got to the twelfth paling there was at least an inch difference in the length of the first and the twelfth palings. Why? Simply because I was following each time a faulty standard, and I increased the difference every time between that and the preceding standard. [1]

Now I want to apply that to this matter. Say there was no standard of text at all—that only the *idea* of the

Bible was inspired, and then we had to have translations, and the translations would be made from translations, and so on as additional copies were needed—by the time we got our tenth translation we would be a thousand miles from the original translation. But in our present translations we don't go back, say, to the King James Version and revise that and put that in more modern English, but each time we make a translation we get just as close back to the original standard as possible, and in this way the translations become a great means for determining the true text.

Suppose we take the Greek translation of the Old Testament. There are several of them—three or four—and we take the Syriac, or Peshito, then the Old Latin translation, the Vulgate, and then the Septuagint translation, and so on throughout the various nations of the world. Every one becomes valuable to us, for each one makes an effort to go back to the true text. We do not try to make a new standard, but try to get back to the original text as nearly as possible, and in that way instead of the deviations increasing as the years roll by, the variations are diminishing. There are less now than there used to be, and if we were to make another translation, say forty years hence, that translation would be nearer the original than the American Standard translation, which we are now using, and of course very much nearer than the King James translation.

Now, that is the reason for having a standard, and it is bound to be a standard of words. The integrity of the text of any book is maintained whenever it is preserved incorrupt, or whenever there are means of restoring anything that is wrong, or making it right again. While we don't maintain that the original text, just as Paul wrote it, or as Peter wrote it, or as Matthew wrote it, or claim that the autograph copy can be shown, yet we do maintain that by the old manuscripts, by the old translations, by the old quotations and by the internal evidence we virtually restore the books of the Bible so that it is just as it was when it was written by the men inspired of God.

Now, one other remark: God's leaving this kind of labor to be performed by man has had a tremendous effect in bringing about a study of the Bible that would never have been undertaken if to every nation there had been handed down, in God's own handwriting, a text of the Bible in their language. If it had been handed down as a solid book from the skies it would not have brought about that reverence for the Bible, that attention to its study that has been accorded it. It would not have called forth that wholesome effect, with sacrifices of toil and money. It would not have engaged the study of so many devout scholars.

These things would not have been, if a Bible had been handed down from heaven in English. So there is nothing in that to interfere with the argument which has been made upon inspiration.

Now I call attention to a general outline of the whole subject that has been presented. It has been stated that to discuss simply the subject of inspiration, it is necessary to assume acquaintance with the text, the canon, and the credibility. All of those, in logical order, go before the subject of inspiration. Taking for granted an acquaintance with the text of the Bible, the canon of the Bible, and the historical credibility of the Bible, I have given no time to the discussion of those subjects, but have assumed that we are taking the Bible as a historical verity with the best of other histories, and that we have the books as they were originally given, and have then discussed the subject of inspiration in the following order:

First: the inspiration of the Scriptures as believed by Baptists from time immemorial.

Second: the question of the inspiration of the Holy Scriptures re-opened.

Third: examples of inspiration and their explanation.

Fourth: Luke's case, and other important matters.

Fifth: certain qualifying facts and the circumstances which modified our ideas of inspiration, enabling us properly to define and limit it.

Sixth: we discussed the difficulties of inspiration and answered certain objections.

Seventh: we took up the book of Daniel as an outstanding example of attack by radical critics.

In these foregoing discussions we have established the inspiration of Jesus Christ, and the inspiration of the New Testament writers.

We then applied the testimony of Christ and His apostles to the Old Testament Scriptures, and when their testimony was applied we learned that they taught the following things:

First: the Old Testament is a single document—the Word of God, the Scriptures; that the Old Testament has been called collectively, as to its books, Sacred books, Holy writings, oracles of God, prophetic writings, the prophecies of Scripture, and titles of that kind.

Then from these general statements Scriptures by Christ were introduced showing that the divisions of the Old Testament are, in general, the Law, the Prophets and the Psalms. Then of every book of the Old Testament clear declarations by these witnesses that every one of the Old Testament writings was inspired of God; and then that the end of this inspiration, or the object in view, was that they might become profitable, and profitable for a definite purpose. All that was presented in the foregoing chapters which I regard as fundamental upon this subject.

Having considered, then, the basis of inspiration, the circumstances were analyzed both in the Old Testament and the New Testament. For instance, a distinction was made between inspiration and other words, such as revelation, which is getting the knowledge of God, while inspiration is accurately stating or recording the knowledge of God; illumination, for the purpose of understanding the statements and records of the knowledge of God, and regeneration and sanctification, for the purpose of harmonizing man with the Word of God.

In this way we brought out the discriminating idea between these terms. Then examples were shown where men were inspired who had no revelation made to them, therefore inspiration and revelation are not identical. Instances also were given where men were inspired who had no illumination, therefore inspiration and illumination are distinct.

The case of the prophets was cited, when they wrote out the words of God and did not know what they meant, and prayed for light on them, and even the angels stooped over from the heavens and tried to look into those things.

We found in the case of Caiaphas that he was not even conscious that he was inspired, supposing that he was speaking his own words, with a wicked intent in his mind, and yet what he said was in a higher sense from God, and had a meaning attached to it different from the meaning in his own mind.

Then examples were shown where men were inspired who were not good men, and examples were shown of inspired men who were good men, but not sanctified men, not *perfectly* good men, and therefore there was no chance, when the matter was properly analyzed, to confound inspiration with revelation, regeneration, sanctification, or illumination.

Finally, as the discussion proceeded, only that part of the inspiration was considered that pertained to the records; that while men were inspired to state what God said as God wished it to be said, we were not present, did not hear those statements, and therefore would not be benefitted unless there was a phase of inspiration that went beyond the mere utterance of the Word of God.

So, in the latter part of the discussions, stress was laid upon the inspiration of the writing—that the Scriptures were God-inspired. The records are inspired, and that is the part of the subject that most nearly concerns us, and that inspiration was an inspiration of the records, which made those records inerrable, not only in idea, but in word. In that case they were written just as God willed them to be written; but while the record was inspired, it did not follow that what the wicked said in that record was inspired of God, or that what the devil said in that word was inspired of God, but the *record of what they said* was inspired of God.

I hope the distinction is clear, because one brother was very much confounded the other day when we were discussing inspiration. He wanted to know if that dumb brute was inspired to speak, if the devil was also inspired to speak in Job and in Matthew.

My reply was that, in both cases, the record was inspired, and the one that prepared the record of the words of the dumb brute was inspired, the one that prepared the record of Job was inspired and the one that prepared the record of the temptation of Christ was inspired, and it seems to me that any intelligent mind could see that.

David committed a grievous sin. The record that tells

us about that is an inspired record, but it doesn't tell us
that God inspired David to commit the sin.

Now, if this record, the discussion went on to show,
is God-inspired, and inerrable, then there must be no
contradiction between the parts. If God inspired the
one hundred and tenth Psalm, and God inspired the
letter to the Hebrews, then the two must be in accord.
They do not fight against each other; and if God inspired Matthew, Mark, Luke, John and Paul to give us
a record of the life and work and office of Jesus Christ,
then Matthew, Mark, Luke, John and Paul must be in
accord. There can be no contradictions between them,
and the position that we take on the matter is that there
are no contradictions in the Bible. We take that stand
openly, not incidentally; advisedly, not ill-advisedly, but
after years of patient study of the subject the stand has
been boldly taken that the books of the Bible are in harmony with each other, and not merely in harmony with
each other, but more than that, the harmony is so vital that
it is not a harmony of mere juxtaposition, which is a mechanical connection, but there is a connection far more than
that—it is a living connection.

For instance, there is no contradiction between the finger
and the ear. They are different, and yet there is a living
connection between them. It is not like a wooden ear and
a wooden finger. There is a living connection the same as
between the eye and the heart, between the hand and the
foot; and as the whole body has a vital connection, so all
the parts of the Bible constitute that living, that quick and
powerful Word of God that abideth forever.

Then the author proceeded to state that inspiration
was closed—that not only was the canon of the Old
Testament completed, but the canon of the New Testament was completed, and if completed, then what follows?

There must be no superfluity, no redundancy. There is not more there than is necessary. There is everything there that is necessary.

There is no superfluity in the Word of God. We cannot trim it down. It does not admit of subtraction, and if it be a complete revelation of God, there are no deficiencies in it—nothing that needs to be filled out. Therefore it is incapable of addition.

We can no more add to it than we can take from it, and if it be a complete revelation, an inspired Bible, then there must be sufficiency in it. By the sufficiency of the Scriptures is meant that they meet all the demands of the case.

There is no possible condition of human nature that can be conceived of by the mind where the Scriptures would fail of sufficient light for the guidance of the man in that condition.

They are all-sufficient.

Not only did this follow, as the discussion showed, but there is efficiency—not merely sufficiency, but efficiency. It is powerful, able to make one wise unto salvation through the Holy Spirit, who inspires the Word of God; is competent for all the purposes contemplated, so that in order to convict a man of sin we need not as a preacher go outside the Word of God to get the means of conviction to regenerate a man; we don't need any testimony beyond the Word of God. They are convicted by the Word of God, or through the Word of God by the Holy Spirit, and therefore when a man goes out to preach, the subject-matter of his preaching is provided for. When he goes out to sow seed, the seed is provided. He is not to mix that with other seed. The sower goes out to sow, and he sows the seed that God provided—the incorruptible seed of the Word—and when he preaches, he preaches the

Word; so the teachings of the Bible are efficient. The man that goes out to represent God as a preacher must preach the things that God says, must preach the Word of God, and no other word.

Now, that doesn't mean that a preacher must not sometimes deliver a Fourth-of-July oration. He may sometimes write a poem, if he wishes, on the stars, on the mists and rainbows of a cascade. That is all right, but he must not expect to convert the world with them.

The efficiency is in God's Word, as well as the sufficiency. There is enough of it there. All of it that is there is needed, and it is very full, too, for it is a live wire. There is no dead wire in it. It is the living Word of God, and is like a two-edged sword, and with the Spirit guiding that sword it can press to the very thoughts and intents of the human heart. Now, all of that is dependent upon its inspiration. This is as far as the discussion has gone.

I will now take up what some people have regarded as an insuperable obstacle in the way of accepting the inspiration of the Scriptures. They say that if the Bible is inspired, and all of its records are accurate, and that there is no errancy in it, then it puts a man of science in the position that he must choose between science and the Bible, their teachings being diverse. [2]

To this man I would say that he is mistaken, and I would challenge him or any other man to show one solitary contradiction between science and the Bible.

But he must confine himself to science.

Science is something known, something proven. He must not bring up his speculative theories, his mental vagaries, and call them science. I challenge him to bring up a single contradiction between the teachings of Scripture and real science.

I have seen that tested on the first chapter of Genesis. That gives an account of the creation of the universe, the formation of the earth, and the creation of man, and to this very day science—not science as represented by some men who try to set the teachings of science over against the Bible by butting their heads against the accounts in Genesis, Job, certain of the Psalms, and Paul's declarations at Athens—but true science is and has ever been in harmony with the Scriptures.

The Word of God stands today grasping the hand of all real science just like the coat-of-arms of the State of Kentucky—" United we stand, divided we fall."

Now I will give you some science: When I was a young fellow, just before the Civil War, a great political emergency arose—the question of slavery—and men not only discussed it from political standpoints, but they began to discuss it from Bible standpoints, and then scientific standpoints, and there was published in the city of New York a daily paper, and because of its peculiar views on the subject of slavery it attained a circulation of many thousands. Just before the war a series of articles was published in that paper to prove that the Negro and the Caucasian, by scientific demonstration, did not have a common origin—that it was impossible in the light of science that all men came from one man.

If that is true, that puts the Bible in default, for if anything in the world is taught in the Bible, it is the unity of the race.

It certainly does teach that the human race descended from Adam, and that the plan of salvation is based upon that fact, and all human redemption is based upon the fact that all these lost descendants of the first Adam are redeemed and saved in the Second Adam.

About this time two doctors, in Mobile, Alabama, who

saw the question from a Southern standpoint, published a very large book, and they contradicted the articles which were published in the New York daily. They saw a conflict between science and the Bible. Well, all that was necessary in that case was not to move the Bible into the scientific camp, but let the Bible stand, and see all the scientists trooping back to get under the Bible-tent; so, I have even lived to see the time come when facts not only prove to the world that scientists are ready to demonstrate the unity of the human race, but that they, like the Indian, stood so straight up that they leaned over, and they went so far as to state that all beings had a common origin—not only man, but monkeys and man; not only monkeys and man, but elephants and man; not only elephants and man, but jellyfish and man; not only jellyfish and man, but cabbage heads and man. Now, all that is necessary is not to move the Bible, but just let it stand.

I have lived to see the theory of Charles Darwin die again as Paul saw it die in its original habitation where it was proclaimed by its advocates in Athens, Corinth and Rome, and today the best advocates of science are just as ready to denounce Darwin as I am.

They say it is not science; and so the Bible goes along like Bunyan's great path, and all along we see roads leading off from it, but they come back again. Some of them cross it at right angles, but then they wind around and come back again. The road goes right on, and about every thirty years we are in harmony with science, because it comes back to us. It plays all around us, first on one side and then on the other, but we need not follow it. We are wasting our time if we try to move the solid foundations of the Bible, so as to accommodate it to the shifting vagaries of science, falsely so-called.

Here comes a marvel. Take any of the accounts of the creation of the world, viz.: the Babylonian, the Egyptian, or that which the Chinese, the Japanese, or the people of Hindustan regard as the origin of the world, and when has there ever been harmony with any scientific fact on that point? It has all the time been confusion.

Now, how was it that a Hebrew away back yonder in the land of Egypt, when all the rest of the world was at sea, if he was not inspired, could write an account of creation that stands and smiles serenely, impervious to every assault of so-called scientific thinking today, as it was then? It is the inspired Word of God.

I have had scientists to bring up that instance of Joshua commanding the sun to stand still. Some preachers skip that chapter, and I am sorry for them. They had better read it just as it is. They had better take it just as it reads.

Only a few weeks ago I saw in a book of great power, an absolute demonstration of what would have been projected as a result if the sun and the moon had stopped, and I have certainly seen it demonstrated that it would not have occurred.

But suppose they put God into the account; if they would just put God in there, that would be a guarantee. He would know how to manage it. I suppose we all believe in an all-powerful God; He could take care of the situation, unless we have a God who finds some things too much for Him. I suppose He could manage that little affair just as He could raise a dead man to life that had gone into corruption.

The great battleground, if we are going to make one of contradictions, is the battleground of the resurrection. Take the testimony of Matthew, Mark, Luke, John and Paul. Now, can any one, from those records, prove either errancy or contradiction in those accounts? I have been over it a great many times, and I freely confess that I see no contradiction in the statements of the witnesses.

I select now a single item which seems to be a positive contradiction in the whole thing. Mark says that Christ was crucified at a certain hour of the day, and John says that He was crucified about six hours later than that. Now, there are the statements with six hours difference. The commentator comes to it, throws down his pen and he says, "There must be some mistake here in the copy. As it stands it is a palpable contradiction."

I have long since found out that a man ought to go slow about affirming a mistake in the copy. I admit that is a possibility, but I don't believe that is the best way to meet this. Can it be reconciled in any other way?

Yes, and there is this explanation of it: Mark wrote as a Jew, and followed the Jewish method of computation, which was from sunrise to sunset and from sunset to sunrise. John followed the Roman method of computation, just exactly as we do. We count from midnight to noon and from noon to midnight. One minute after twelve o'clock, midnight, is A. M.

"Well," says one, "if this is true, that will harmonize it exactly, but what is your evidence that John employed the Roman method?"

My evidence is fully set forth in his Gospel. He used the Roman hour, and some of the cases absolutely demand it. All we have to do is to take the Gospel of John, go through it and see where he refers to hours.

That, of course, is met by the statement that the Romans did not use that method, and we simply meet that by proving that they did use it, and at least five of the best Roman historians state that they did.

But the question comes up: Why should John employ

that method and not the others? The answer is that the others wrote before the destruction of Jerusalem, before the Jewish nation had been blotted out by that fearful catastrophe. John wrote many years after Jerusalem was destroyed, when the Jewish method of computation no longer governed anywhere. The time that he wrote in Ephesus was about the year 90, or later, which would be at least twenty years after the destruction of Jerusalem, and it was the most natural thing in the world that all through his Gospel he should have employed the Roman method; and I can cite some passages in John where you are compelled to have it.

I have seen these contradictions melt away until I have lost all confidence in them. Now, a boy is usually a great deal smarter than his father, and than he is when he gets to be a father. When I was a boy I thought I had found a thousand contradictions in the Bible. In the old Bible of my young manhood I marked them.

Well, I had then nearly a thousand more contradictions than I have now. I do not see them now; they are not there. There are perhaps a half dozen in the Bible that I cannot explain satisfactorily to myself. I don't say that my explanation of all the others would satisfy everybody. There are some that I cannot explain satisfactorily to myself; but since I have seen nine hundred and ninety-four out of the thousand coalesce and harmonize like two streams mingling, I am disposed to think that if I had more sense I could harmonize those other six; and even if I forever fail to harmonize them, God knows better than I know, and that when I know perfectly just as I now know only in part, and only a very small part, I will be able to understand that; and so when I come to things of that kind and cannot master them, I put them in a parenthesis and say, " I will come back; God won't leave you penned forever; He will send somebody that can take away the difficulty and make it clear to me." I assume that it can be done.

The President of the State University once remarked about a noted infidel in Waco, that his infidelity arose from this: He had read a book against the Bible which he could not answer, and he concluded that as it was a book he could not answer, it was unanswerable, and it is the best explanation I ever heard of that man. He is just the kind of man that would assume that anything he could not solve was unsolvable.

We will not take that position. We need to get away from such conceit. Believing that we have an infallible standard, we will go on like the old-time Baptists, who put it in their articles of faith, and we can do nothing better than to close this last chapter with the same quotation from our Confession of Faith with which the first chapter was introduced:

" We believe that the Holy Bible was written by men divinely inspired, and is a perfect treasure of heavenly instruction; that it has God for its author, salvation for its end, and truth without any mixture of error for its matter; that it reveals the principles by which God will judge us; and therefore is, and shall remain to the end of the world, the true center of Christian union, and the supreme standard by which all human conduct, creeds, and opinions shall be tried."

NOTES

1. Dr. Carroll's answer to those who deny the concept of the perfection of Scripture based upon the absence of the autographs is vividly portrayed in this illustration. Textual critics may labor with stellar success, discovering the precise wording of a text. However, all such labor pays questionable dividends if all one discovers is the fallible witness of another mortal. On the other hand, if the Scriptures were given inerrantly from the heart of God, the discovery of what Paul or John actually wrote is the discovery of precise revelation as it came from God. (Patterson)

2. Note that Carroll speaks here of "errancy." This demonstrates that he was aware of the allegations of "error" in the Bible. Though he did not use the word "inerrancy," a term that had not yet gained currency in the Baptist life of Carroll's era, this paragraph makes it amply lucid that he would not have hesitated to use the word. (Patterson)

APPENDIX

MY INFIDELITY AND WHAT BECAME OF IT*

A Sermon by B. H. Carroll

I CANNOT remember when I began to be an infidel. Certainly at a very early age—even before I knew what infidelity meant. There was nothing in my home life to beget or suggest it. My father was a self-educated Baptist minister, preaching—mainly without compensation—to village or country churches. My mother was a devoted Christian of deep and humble piety. There were no infidel books in our home library, nor in any other accessible to me. My teachers were Christians—generally preachers. There were no infidels of my acquaintance, and no public sentiment in favor of them. My infidelity was never from without, but always from within. I had no precept and no example. When, later in life, I read infidel books, they did not make me an infidel, but because I was an infidel I sought, bought, and read them. Even when I read them I was not impressed by new suggestions, but only when occasionally they gave clearer expression of what I had already vaguely felt. No one of them nor all of them sounded the depths of my own infidelity or gave an adequate expression of it. They all fell short of the distance in doubt over which my own troubled soul had passed.

From unremembered time this skepticism progressed, though the progress was not steady and regular. Sometimes in

*This account was first given in an address at Nashville, Tenn. and by request of Dr. J. M. Frost was reported for the "Teacher" of the Southern Baptist Convention S. S. Series.

125

one hour, as by far-shining flashes of inspiration, there would be more progress in extent and definiteness than in previous months. Moreover, these short periods of huge advances were without preceding intentions or perceptible preparations. They were always sudden and startling. Place and circumstances had but little to do with them. The doubt was seldom germane to the topic under consideration. It always leaped far away to a distant and seemingly disconnected theme, in a way unexplained by the law of the association of ideas. At times I was in the Sunday-school or hearing a sermon or bowed with others in family prayer—more frequently when I waked at night after healthful sleep, and still more frequently when rambling alone in the fields or in the woods. To be awake in the stillness of the night while others slept, or to be alone in forest depths, or on boundless prairies, or on mountain heights has always possessed for me a weird fascination. Even to this day there are times when houses and people are unbearable. Frequently have I been intoxicated with thoughts of the immensity of space and the infinity of nature. Now these were the very times when skepticism made such enormous progress. "When I consider thy heavens, the work of thy fingers, the moon and the stars which thou hast ordained; what is man, that thou art mindful of him, and the son of man, that thou visitest him."

Thus, before I knew what infidelity was, I was an infidel. My child-mind was fascinated by strange and sometimes horrible questionings concerning many religious subjects. Long before I had read the experiences of others, I had been borne far beyond sight of any shore, wading and swimming beyond my depth after solutions to such questions as the "philosopher's stone," the "elixir of life," and "the fountain of youth," but mainly the "chief good." I understand now much better than then the character and direction of the questionings of that early period. By a careful restrospect and analysis of such of them as memory preserves, I now know that I never doubted the being, personality, and government of God. I was never an atheist or pantheist. I never doubted the existence and ministry of angels—pure spirits never embodied: I could never have been a Sadducee. I never doubted the essential distinction between spirit and matter: I could never have been a materialist.

And as to the origin of things, the philosophy of Democritus, developed by Epicurus, more developed by Lucretius, and gone to seed in the unverified hypothesis of modern evolutionists—such a godless, materialistic anti-climax of philosophy never had the slightest attraction or temptation for me. The intuitions of humanity preserved me from any ambition to be descended from either beast or protoplasm. The serious reception of such a speculative philosophy was not merely a mental, but mainly a moral impossibility. I never doubted the immortality of the soul and conscious future existence. This conviction antedated any reading of "Plato, thou reasonest well." I never doubted the final, just judgment of the Creator of the world.

But my infidelity related to the Bible and its manifest doctrines. I doubted that it was God's book; that it was an inspired revelation of his will to man. I doubted miracles. I doubted the divinity of Jesus of Nazareth. But more than all, I doubted his vicarious expiation for the sins of men. I doubted any real power and vitality in the Christian religion. I never doubted that the Scriptures claimed inspiration, nor that they taught unequivocally the divinity and vicarious expiation of Jesus. If the Bible does not teach these, it teaches nothing. The trifling expedient of accepting the Bible as "inspired in spots," never occurred to me. To accept, with Renan, its natural parts and arbitrarily deny its supernatural, or to accept with some the book as from God, and then strike at its heart by a false interpretation that denied the divinity and vicarious expiation of Jesus—these were follies of which I was never guilty—follies for which even now I have never seen or heard a respectable excuse. To me it was always *"Aut Cæsar, aut nihil."* What anybody wanted, in a religious way, with the shell after the kernel was gone I never could understand.

While the beginnings of my infidelity cannot be recalled, by memory I can give the date when it took tangible shape. I do know just when it emerged from chaos and outlined itself in my consciousness with startling distinctness. An event called it out of the mists and shadows into conscious reality. It happened on this wise:

There was a protracted meeting in our vicinity. A great and mysterious influence swept over the community. There was much excitement. Many people, old and young, joined the church and were baptized. Doubtless in the beginning of the meeting the conversions were what I would now call genuine. Afterward many merely went with the tide. They went because others were going. Two things surprised me. First, that I did not share the interest or excitement. To me it was only a curious spectacle. The second was that so many people wanted me to join the church. I had manifested no special interest except once or twice mechanically and experimentally. I had no conviction for sin. I had not felt lost and did not feel saved. First one and then another catechised me, and that categorically. Thus: "Don't you believe the Bible?" "Yes." "Don't you believe in Jesus Christ?" "Y-e-s." "Well, doesn't the Bible say that whosoever believes in Jesus Christ is saved?" "Yes." Now, mark three things: First, this catechising was by zealous church-members before I presented myself for membership. Second, the answers were historical, Sunday-school answers, as from a text-book. Third, I was only thirteen years old. These answers were reported to the preachers somewhat after this fashion: "Here is a lad who believes the Bible, believes in Jesus Christ, and believes that he is saved. Ought not such a one to join the church?" Now came the pressure of well-meant but unwise persuasion. I will not describe it. The whole thing would have been exposed if, when I presented myself for membership, I had been asked to tell my own story without prompting or leading questions. I did not have any to tell, and would have told none. But many had joined, the hour was late, and a few direct questions elicited the same historical, stereotyped answers. Thus the die was cast.

Until after my baptism everything seemed unreal, but walking home from the baptism the revelation came. The vague infidelity of all the past took positive shape, and would not down at my bidding. Truth was naked before me. My answers had been educational. I did not believe that the Bible was God's revelation. I did not believe its miracles and doctrines. I did not believe, in any true sense, in the divinity or vicarious sufferings of Jesus. I had no confidence in professed conversion and regeneration. I had not felt lost nor did I feel saved. There was no perceptible, radical change in my disposition or affections. What I once loved, I still loved; what I once hated, I still hated. It was no temporary depression of spirit following a previous exaltation, such as I now believe sometimes comes to genuine Christians. This I knew. Joining the church, with its assumption of obligations, was a touchstone. It acted on me like the touch of Ithuriel's spear. I saw my real self. I knew that either I had no religion or it was not worth having. This certainty as to my state had no intermittence. The sensation of actual and positive infidelity was so new to me that I hardly knew what to say about it. I felt a repugnance to parade it. I wanted time and trial for its verification. I knew that its avowal would pain and horrify my family and the church, yet honesty required me to say something. And so I merely asked that the church withdraw from me on the ground that I was not converted. This was not granted, because the brethren thought that I mistook temporary mental depression for lack of conversion. They asked me to wait and give it a trial; to read the Bible and pray. I could not make them understand, but from that time on I read the Bible as never before—read it all; read it many times; studied it in the light of my infidelity; marked its contradictions and fallacies, as they seemed to me, from Genesis to Revelation. Two years passed away. In this interval we moved to Texas. In a meeting in Texas, when I was fifteen years old, I was persuaded to retain membership for further examination. Now came the period of reading Christian apologies and infidel books. What a multitude of them of both kinds! Hume, Paine, Volney, Bolingbroke, Rousseau, Voltaire, Taylor, Gibbon, *et al*, over against Watson, Nelson, Horn, Calvin, Walker, and a host of others. In the meantime I was at college, devouring the Greek, Roman, and Oriental philosophies. At seventeen, being worn out in body and mind, I joined McCullough's Texas Rangers, the first regiment mustered into the Confederate service, and on the remote, uninhabited frontier pursued the investigation with unabated ardor.

But now came another event. I shall not name it. It came from no sin on my part, but it blasted every hope and left me in Egyptian darkness. The battle of life was lost. In seeking the field of war, I sought death. By peremptory demand I had my church connection dissolved, and turned utterly away from every semblance of Bible belief. In the hour of my darkness I turned unreservedly to infidelity. This time I brought it a broken heart and a disappointed life, asking for light and peace and rest. It was now no curious speculation; no tentative intellectual examination. It was a stricken soul, tenderly and anxiously and earnestly seeking light. As I was in the first Confederate regiment, so I was in the last corps that surrendered; but while armies grappled and throttled each other, a darker and deadlier warfare raged within me. I do know this: my quest for the truth was sincere and unintermittent. Happy people whose lives are not blasted, may affect infidelity, may appeal to its oracles from a curious, speculative interest, and may minister to their intellectual pride by seeming to be odd. It was not so with me. With all the earnestness of a soul between which and happiness the bridges were burned, I brought a broken and bleeding, but honest heart to every reputed oracle of infidelity. I did not ask life or fame or pleasure. I merely asked light to shine on the path of right. Once more I viewed the anti-Christian philosophies, no longer to admire them in what they destroyed, but to inquire what they built up, what they offered to a hungry heart and a blasted life. There now came to me a revelation as awful as when Mokanna, in Moore's "Lalla Rookh," lifted his veil for Zelica.

Why had I never seen it before? How could I have been blind to it? These philosophies, one and all, were mere negations. They were destructive, but not constructive. They overturned and overturned and overturned; but, as my soul liveth, they built up nothing under the whole heaven in the place of what they destroyed. I say nothing; I mean nothing. To the unstricken, curious soul, they are as beautiful as the aurora borealis, shining on arctic icebergs. But to me they warmed nothing and melted nothing. No flowers bloomed and no fruit ripened under their cheerless beams. They looked down on my bleeding heart as the cold, distant, pitiless stars have ever looked down on all human suffering. Whoever, in his hour of real need, makes abstract philosophy his pillow, makes cold, hard granite his pillow. Whoever looks trustingly into any of its false faces, looks into the face of a Medusa, and is turned to stone. They are all wells without water, and clouds without rain. I have witnessed a drouth in Texas. The earth was iron and the heavens brass. Dust clouded the thoroughfares and choked the travelers. Water courses ran dry, grass scorched and crackled, corn leaves twisted and wilted, stock died around the last water holes, the ground cracked in fissures, and the song of birds died out in parched throats. Men despaired. The whole earth prayed: "Rain, rain, rain! O heaven, send rain!" Suddenly a cloud rises above the horizon and floats into vision like an angel of hope. It spreads a cool shade over the burning and glowing earth. Expectation gives life to desire. The lowing herds look up. The shriveled flowers open their tiny cups. The corn leaves untwist and rustle with gladness. And just when all trusting, suffering life opens her confiding heart to the promise of relief, the cloud, the cheating cloud, like a heartless coquette, gathers her drapery about her and floats scornfully away, leaving the angry sun free to dart his fires of death into the open heart of all suffering life. Such a cloud without rain is any form of infidelity to the soul in its hour of need.

Who then can conjure by the name of Voltaire? Of what avail in that hour is Epicurus or Zeno, Huxley or Darwin? Here now was my case: I had turned my back on Christianity, and had found nothing in infidelity; happiness was gone, and death would not come. The Civil War had left me a wounded cripple on crutches, utterly poverty-stricken and loaded with debt. The internal war of infidelity, after making me roll hopelessly the ever-falling stone of Sisyphus, vainly climb the revolving wheel of Ixion, and stoop like Tantalus to drink waters that ever receded, or reach out for fruit that could not be grasped, now left me bound like Prometheus on the cold rock, while vultures tore with beak and talons a life that could suffer, but could not die.

At this time two books of the Bible took hold of me with unearthly power. I had not a thought of their inspiration, but I knew from my experience that they were neither fiction nor allegory—the book of Job and the book of Ecclesiastes. Some soul had walked those paths. They were histories; not dreams and not mere poems. Like Job, I believed in God; and like him, had cried: "Oh that I knew where I might find him! that I might come even to his seat! . . . Behold, I go forward, but he is not there; and backward, but I cannot perceive him: on the left hand, where he doth work, but I cannot behold him: he hideth himself on the right hand, that I cannot see him: but he knoweth the way that I take." Like Job, I could not find answers in nature to the heart's sorest need and the most important questions; and, like Job, regarding God as my adversary, I had cried out for a revelation: "Oh that one would hear me! behold, my desire is, that the Almighty would answer me, and that mine adversary had written a book. Surely I would take it upon my shoulder, and bind it as a crown to me." Like Job, I felt the need of a mediator, who as a man could enter into my case, and as divine could enter into God's case; and, like Job, I had complained: "He is not a man, as I am, that I should answer him, and we should come together in judgment. Neither is there any daysman betwixt us, that might lay his hand upon us both." And thus I approached my twenty-second year.

I had sworn never to put my foot in another church. My father had died believing me lost. My mother—when does a mother give up a child?—came to me one day and begged, for her sake, that I would attend one more meeting. It was a Methodist camp meeting, held in the fall of 1865. I had not an atom of interest in it. I liked the singing, but the preaching did not touch me. But one day I shall never forget. It was Sunday at 11 o'clock. The great, wooden shed was crowded. I stood on the outskirts, leaning on my crutches, wearily and some-what scornfully enduring. The preacher made a failure even for him. There was nothing in his sermon. But when he came down, as I supposed to exhort as usual, he startled me not only by not exhorting, but by asking some questions that seemed meant for me. He said: "You that stand aloof from

Christianity and scorn us simple folks, what have you got? Answer honestly before God, have you found anything worth having where you are?" My heart answered in a moment: "Nothing under the whole heaven; absolutely nothing." As if he had heard my unspoken answer, he continued: "Is there anything else out there worth trying, that has any promise in it?" Again my heart answered: "Nothing; absolutely nothing. I have been to the jumping-off place on all these roads. They all lead to a bottomless abyss." "Well, then," he continued, "admitting there's nothing there, if there be a God, mustn't there be a something somewhere? If so, how do you know it is not here? Are you willing to test it? Have you the fairness and courage to try it? I don't ask you to read any book, nor study any evidences, nor make any difficult and tedious pilgrimages; that way is too long and time is too short. Are you willing to try it now: to make a practical, experimental test, you to be the judge of the result?" These cool, calm, and pertinent questions hit me with tremendous force, but I didn't understand the test. He continued: "I base my test on these two scriptures: 'If any man willeth to do his will, he shall know of the doctrine whether it be of God;' 'Then shall we know if we follow on to know the Lord.' " For the first time I understood the import of these scriptures. I had never before heard of such a translation for the first and had never examined the original text. In our version it says: "If any man will do the will of God, he shall know of the doctrine whether it be of God." But the preacher quoted it: "Whosoever willeth to do the will of God," showing that the knowledge as to whether the doctrine was of God depended not upon external action and not upon exact conformity with God's will, but upon the internal disposition—"whosoever willeth or wishes to do God's will." The old translation seemed to make knowledge impossible; the new, practicable. In the second scripture was also new light: "Then shall we know if we follow on to know the Lord," which means that true knowledge follows persistence in the prosecution of it—that is, it comes not to temporary and spasmodic investigation.

So, when he invited all who were willing to make an immediate experimental test to come forward and give him their hands, I immediately went forward. I was not prepared for the stir which this action created. My infidelity and my hostile attitude toward Christianity were so well known in the community that such action on my part developed quite a sensation. Some even began to shout. Whereupon, to prevent any misconception, I arose and stated that I was not converted, that perhaps they misunderstood what was meant by my coming forward; that my heart was as cold as ice; my action meant no more than that I was willing to make an experimental test of the truth and power of the Christian religion, and that I was willing to persist in subjection to the test until a true solution could be found. This quieted matters.

The meeting closed without any change upon my part. The last sermon had been preached, the benediction pronounced, and the congregation was dispersing. A few ladies only remained, seated near the pulpit and engaged in singing. Feeling that the experiment was ended and the solution not found, I remained to hear them sing. As their last song, they sang:

> O land of rest, for thee I sigh,
>   When will the moment come
> When I shall lay my armor by
>   And dwell in peace at home.

The singing made a wonderful impression upon me. Its tones were as soft as the rustling of angels' wings. Suddenly there flashed upon my mind, like a light from heaven, this scripture: "Come unto me all ye that labor and are heavy laden, and I will give you rest." I did not see Jesus with my eye, but I seemed to see him standing before me, looking reproachfully and tenderly and pleadingly, seeming to rebuke me for having gone to all other sources for rest but the right one, and now inviting me to come to him. In a moment I went, once and forever, casting myself unreservedly and for all time at Christ's feet, and in a moment the rest came, indescribable and unspeakable, and it has remained from that day until now.

I gave no public expression of the change which had passed over me, but spent the night in the enjoyment of it and wondering if it would be with me when morning came. When the morning came it was still with me, brighter than the sunlight and sweeter than the song of birds, and now, for the first time, I understood the scripture which I had often heard my mother repeat: "Ye shall go out with joy, and be led forth with peace: the mountains and the hills shall break forth before you into singing, and all the trees of the field shall clap their hands" (Isa. 55:12).

When I reached home, I said nothing about the experience through which I had passed, hiding the righteousness of God in my own heart; but it could not be hidden. As I was walking across the floor on my crutches, an orphan boy whom my mother had raised, noticed and called attention to the fact that I was both whistling and crying. I knew that my mother heard him, and, to avoid observation, I went at once to my room, lay down on the bed, and covered my face with my hands. I heard her coming. She pulled my hands away from my face and gazed long and steadfastly upon me without a word. A light came over her face that made it seem to me as the shining on the face of Stephen; and then, with trembling lips, she said; "My son, you have found the Lord." Her happiness was indescribable. I don't think she slept that night. She seemed to fear that with sleep she might dream and wake to find that the glorious fact was but a vision of the night. I spent the night at her bedside reading Bunyan's "Pilgrim's Progress." I read it all that night, and when I came with the pilgrims to the Beulah Land, from which Doubting Castle could be seen no more forever, and which was in sight of the heavenly city and within sound of the heavenly music, my soul was filled with such a rapture and such an ecstacy of joy as I had never before experienced. I knew then as well as I know now that I would preach; that it would be my life-work; that I would have no other work.